▲▲▲

Day and Overnight Hikes in West Virginia's Monongahela National Forest

Other Books By Johnny Molloy

▼▼▼

Best In Tent Camping: West Virginia

Trail By Trail: Backpacking in the Smoky Mountains

Day & Overnight Hikes
in the Great Smoky Mountains National Park

Best In Tent Camping: Smoky Mountains

Best In Tent Camping: Florida

Day & Overnight Hikes
in the Shenandoah National Park

Beach & Coastal Camping in Florida

Best In Tent Camping: Colorado

A Paddler's Guide to Everglades National Park

Day and Overnight HIKES
in West Virginia's
MONONGAHELA
National Forest

▲▲▲

by Johnny Molloy

Menasha Ridge Press
Birmingham, Alabama

Cover design by Grant Tatum
Cover photograph by Dennis Coello
Text design by Carolina Graphics Group
Maps by inkspot a design co.

Cataloging-in-Publication Data

Molloy, Johnny, 1961-
    Day and overnight hikes in West Virginia's Monongahela National
Forest / by Johnny Molloy.
            p.   cm.
    Includes bibliographical reference and index.
    ISBN 0-89732-318-1
    1. Hiking—West Virginia—Monongahela National Forest—
Guidebooks. 2. Monongahela National Forest (W. Va.)—
Guidebooks. I. Title.
    GV191.42.W42 M666 2000
    917.54'85—dc21   00-021694
                                                CIP

Menasha Ridge Press
700 28th Street, Suite 206
Birmingham, Alabama 35233
www.menasharidge.com

Table Of Contents

This book is for my long time friend,
Francisco Meyer.

▲▲▲

Acknowledgments

Thanks to the following folks for help in making this book a reality: Rick Arnold and Ann Blackmon at Richwood; Martin Miller and Bryan Delay for going backpacking with me; and Tinian Molloy for taking pains to ship me a computer when my laptop broke down. Thanks to Cisco Meyer for watching over the Fort, and Deal Holcomb for helping with the old Jeep. And Steele, Pat and Nelle Molloy for helping with new Jeep. Thanks to Budd Zehmer for the idea and everyone at Menasha for following through. Thanks to all the folks I met on the trail and around the mountains of West Virginia. They made my time in the Mountain State so wonderful.

Preface

The Monongahela National Forest, located entirely within West Virginia, is the heart and soul of the wild, wonderful Mountain State. The numbers are as follows: 900,000 acres of land with elevations ranging from 900 to 4,862 feet, including Spruce Knob—the highest point in the state; 600 miles of cold-water fisheries, including 90% of the native brook trout waters in the state, 130 miles of warm-water fisheries; nearly 80,000 acres of designated wilderness, over 75 tree species, and more than 800 miles of hiking trails.

Formed in 1920, the "Mon" is more than numbers. It is a natural getaway for native mountaineers and outdoor enthusiasts from the Mid-Atlantic metropoli, as well it should be. Climbers can scale Seneca Rocks, auto tourists can enjoy the vistas of the Highlands Scenic Highway, mountain bikers can pedal Canaan Mountain, campers can spend the night at any of the campgrounds scattered throughout the forest, and hikers can enjoy the forest from the Dolly Sods up north to way down south near Lake Sherwood.

The first trails were made by Indians who camped along the valleys of the major rivers here—the Cheat, the Tygart, the Greenbrier, and the Potomac. Later, these nomadic natives formed more permanent communities, which were the genesis of tribes such as the Seneca. These tribes suffered the same fate as most North American Indians, as the fertile valleys became settled by pioneers spreading West over the Alleghenies. The high forests remained mostly untouched until after West Virginia became a state during the Civil War. Battles were fought on what later became National Forest land, to control passes through the rugged mountains. A notable battle occurred over Cheat Summit Fort, where Robert E. Lee himself failed to wrestle the stronghold from Union hands. And so the western part of the Old Dominion became independent.

America expanded and the need for wood increased. The spread of the railroad and high-speed band saws opened the mountains of West Virginia to removal of vast stands of virgin woodland. Within 30 years, much of the state was cut over. Then the floods came because there was no vegetation to absorb and slow waters flowing from the mountains. This watery devastation of the lowlands, particularly the flood of 1907, led to the creation of the Monongahela National Forest. Federal management of these lands could result in watershed protection among other things.

There was much work to do: replanting trees, and cutting roads and trails. At first, the work was slow. Many mountaineers resented the presence of the "Feds" in their backyard. Ironically, it was the Great Depression that sped the evolution of the forest. Many young men, unable to find jobs, joined the Civilian Conservation Corps, which established work camps throughout the Monongahela. For nearly ten years they made a mark on the forest. To this day, you can see their handiwork at campgrounds like Blue Bend.

The forest began to recover. Through wildlife management programs, native species of the Alleghenies began to thrive. White-tailed deer lingered on the edge of clearings, and black bears furtively fed on fall's mast. Other smaller critters, from salamanders to falcons, called the wooded ridges and valleys home.

And now humans, as recreationalists, can return to a grand forest once again to fish for secretive brook trout, to listen to the wind whistle through highland spruce woods, to identify a tiny but colorful wildflower, to see the changing of the seasons from a grand rock vista. But to best enjoy the "Mon" you must take to your feet. The rewards increase with every footfall beneath the stately cherry trees of the ridgetops or into valleys of rhododendron where waterfalls roar among misted woodlands.

The Monongahela has undergone many changes, but through it all these hills have shone. There is much to see and little time to see it all in our hurried era. But a respite into the mountains will revitalize both mind and spirit. To smell the autumn leaves on a crisp afternoon, to climb to a lookout, to contemplate pioneer lives at an old homestead will put our lives into perspective.

That is where this book will come into play. It will help you make every step count, whether you are leading the family on a brief day hike or undertaking a challenging backpack into the remote reaches of the forest. With your precious time and the knowledge imparted to you, your outdoor experience will be realized to its fullest.

Often, forest sight-seers randomly pick a hike not knowing where it will lead, or they follow the crowds wherever they go. Many times, I've been stopped with the question, "What's down this trail?" Choosing a hike at random in the sizable Monongahela, where many paths drop or climb steeply, may result in a rigorous affair with no rewards to show for the effort.

This book presents more than 30 day hikes from which to choose. Included are some of the classics such as High Falls and Seneca Rocks. However, the majority of hikes are off the beaten path, offering more solitude to lesser known—yet equally scenic— sights such as Canyon Rim and Meadow Mountain. This will give you the opportunity to get back to nature on your own terms.

Two types of day hikes are offered: one-way and loop hikes. One-way hikes lead to a particular rewarding destination, returning via the same trail. The return trip allows you to see everything from the opposite vantage point. You may notice more minute trailside features the second go-round, and returning at a different time of day may give the same path a surprisingly different character. But to some, returning on the same trail just isn't as enjoyable. Some hikers just can't stand the thought of covering the same ground twice with 800 miles of Monongahela trails awaiting them. The loop hikes provide an alternative.

Most of these hikes offer solitude to maximize your Monongahela experience. It should also be noted that loop hikes are generally longer and more difficult than one-way hikes, but a bigger challenge can reap bigger rewards.

Day hiking is the best and most popular way to "break into" the national forest. But for those with the inclination to see the mountain cycle from day to night and back again, this book offers ten overnight loop hikes with the best locales for camping. The length of these hikes—three days and two nights—was chosen primarily for the weekend backpacker. Backpackers must follow forest regulations and practice "Leave No Trace" wilderness-use etiquette.

When touring the Monongahela, it's a great temptation to remain in your car to enjoy the sights along the forest roads. While auto touring is a great way to get an overview of the forest, it creates a barrier between you and the wilderness beyond. Windshield tourists hoping to observe wildlife often end up observing only the traffic around them. While overlooks provide easy views, the hassle of driving, the drone of traffic, and the lack of effort in reaching the views can make them less than inspirational. The "Mon" is great for hiking.

The wilderness experience can unleash your mind and body, allowing you to relax and find peace and quiet. It also enables you to grasp beauty and splendor: a white-quartz outcrop with a window overlooking the patchwork valley below, a bobcat disappearing into a laurel thicket, or a snow-covered clearing marking an old homestead. In these untamed lands you can let your mind roam—free to go where it pleases. This simply cannot be achieved in a climate-controlled automobile.

The next sections offer advice on how to use this book and how to have a safe and pleasant hike in the woods. The Monongahela is one of West Virginia's special natural resources—get out and enjoy it.

—Johnny Molloy

Introduction

How to Use This Guidebook

At the top of the section for each hike is a box that allows the hiker quick access to pertinent information: quality of scenery, condition of trail, appropriateness for children, difficulty of hike, quality of solitude expected, distance, approximate time of hike, and highlights of the trip. The first five categories are rated using a five-star system. Below is an example of a box included with a hike:

Upper Red Creek

Scenery: ★★★★★
Difficulty: ★★
Trail Condition: ★★★★
Solitude: ★★★
Children: ★★★
Distance: 5.8 miles round-trip
Hiking Time: 3:45 round-trip
Outstanding Features: extraordinary vistas from grassy plains

The five stars indicate the scenery is very picturesque, the trail conditions are fairly good (one star and the trail is likely to be muddy, rocky, overgrown or have some obstacle), the hike is doable for able-bodied children (a one-star rating would denote that only the most gung ho and physically fit children should go). The two stars indicate it will be a relatively easy hike (five stars for difficulty would be strenuous) and you can expect to run into only a few people (with one star you may well be elbowing your way up the trail).

Distances given are absolute, but hiking times are estimated for the average hiker making a round-trip. Overnight loop hiking times include the burden of carrying a pack. Following each box is a brief description of the hike. A more detailed account follows, in which trail junctions, stream crossings, and trailside features are noted along with their distance from the trailhead. This should help you keep apprised of your whereabouts as well as ensure that you don't miss those features noted. You can use this guidebook to walk just a portion of a hike or to plan a hike of your own by combining the information.

The hikes have been divided into one-way day hikes, loop day hikes, and overnight loop hikes. Each type of hike is separated into three general scenic areas of the Monongahela National Forest. The Dolly Sods-Otter Creek area is in the northern area of the national forest. The Spruce Knob-Laurel Fork area is in the north-central forest. The Cranberry area is in the forest's most southerly lands. Feel free to flip through the book, read the descriptions, and choose a hike that appeals to you.

Weather

Each of the four distinct seasons lay its hands on the Monongahela National Forest, though elevation always factors into forest weather patterns. While each season brings exciting changes in the flora and fauna, though the changes can occur seemingly day-to-day rather than month-to-month.

Be prepared for a wide range of temperatures and conditions regardless of the season. As a rule of thumb, the temperature decreases about three degrees with every 1,000 feet of elevation gained. Rainfall varies between 35 and 60 inches annually. This precipitation is evenly distributed throughout the year, though it arrives with slow-moving frontal systems in winter and with thunderstorms in summer.

Spring is the most variable season. During March, you'll find your first signs of rebirth in the lowlands, yet trees in the high country may not be fully leafed out until June. Both winter- and summer-like weather can be experienced in spring. As summer approaches, the strong fronts weaken, and thunderstorms and haze become more frequent. Summertime rainy days can be cool. In fall, continental fronts once again sweep through, clearing the air and bringing warm days and cool nights, though rain is always possible.

The first snows of winter usually arrive in November and snow can intermittently fall through April, though no permanent snowpack exists. About 40 to 120 inches of snow can fall during this time. Expect to incur entire days of below-freezing weather, though temperatures can range from mild to bitterly cold.

Clothing

There is a wide variety from which to choose. Basically, use common sense and be prepared for anything. If all you have are cotton clothes when a sudden rainstorm comes along, you'll be miserable, especially in cooler weather. It's a good idea to carry along a light wool sweater or some type of synthetic apparel (polypropylene, Capeline, Thermax, etc.) as well as a hat.

Always carry raingear. Thunderstorms can come on suddenly in the summer, and winter fronts can soak you to the bone. Keep in mind that rainy days are as much a part of nature as those idyllic ones you desire. Besides, rainy days really cut down on the crowds. With appropriate raingear, a normally crowded trail can be a wonderful place of solitude. Do, however, remember that getting wet opens the door to hypothermia.

Footwear is another concern. Though tennis shoes may be appropriate for paved areas, many Monongahela National Forest trails are rocky and rough; tennis shoes may not offer enough support. Boots, waterproofed or not, should be your footwear of choice. Sport sandals are more popular than ever, but these leave much of your foot exposed. An injured foot far from the trailhead can make for a miserable limp back to the car.

Safety Concerns

To some potential mountain enthusiasts, the deep woods seem inordinately dark and perilous. It is the fear of the unknown that causes this anxiety. No doubt, potentially dangerous situations can occur in the outdoors, but as long as you use sound judgment and prepare yourself before hitting the trail, you'll be much safer in the woods than most urban areas of the country. It is better to look at a backcountry hike as a fascinating chance to discover the unknown, rather than a chance for potential disaster. Here are a few tips to make your trip safer and easier:

- Always carry food and water whether you are going overnight or not. Food will give you energy, help keep you warm, and may sustain you in an emergency situation until help arrives. You never know if you will have a stream nearby when you become thirsty. Bring potable water or treat water before drinking it from a stream. The chance of getting sick from the organism known as giardia or other waterborne organisms is small, but there is no reason to take that chance. Boil or filter all water before drinking it.

- Stay on designated trails. Most hikers get lost when they leave the path. If you become disoriented, don't panic—that may result in a bad decision that will make your predicament worse. Retrace your steps if you can remember them or stay where you are. Rangers check the trails first when searching for lost or overdue hikers. Because the Monongahela is a high elevation forest, following a creek or drainage downstream should lead you to the civilized world.

- Bring a map, compass, and lighter, and know how to use them. Should you become lost, these three items can keep you around long enough to be found or get yourself out of a pickle. A compass can help you orient yourself, and a lighter can start a fire for signaling help or keeping warm. Trail maps are available at ranger stations or visitor centers.

- Be especially careful crossing streams. Whether you are fording the stream or crossing on a log, make every step count. If you have any doubt about maintaining your balance on a foot log, go ahead and ford the stream instead. When fording a stream, use a stout tree limb or cane for balance, and face upstream as you cross. If a stream seems too deep to ford, turn back. Whatever is on the other side is not worth risking your life.

- Be careful at overlooks. The national forest has numerous bluffs and outcrops. While these areas may provide spectacular views, they are potentially hazardous. Stay back from the edge of outcrops and be absolutely sure of your footing; a misstep can mean a nasty and possibly fatal fall.

- Know the symptoms of hypothermia. Shivering and forgetfulness are the two most common indicators of this cold-weather killer. Hypothermia can occur at higher elevations, even in the summer, especially when the hiker is wearing lightweight cotton clothing. If symptoms arise, get the victim shelter, hot liquids, and dry clothes or a dry sleeping bag.

- Avoid bear-fear paralysis. The black bears of the Monongahela National Forest are wild animals, hence they are unpredictable. If you see one, give it a wide berth and don't feed it and you'll be fine. There has never been a recorded death caused by a bear in the Mon; most injuries have occurred when an ignorant visitor fed or otherwise harassed a wild bear. So don't stay in your car for fear of bears, just give them plenty of respect.

- Take along your brain. A cool, calculating mind is the single most important piece of equipment you'll ever need on the trail. Think before you act. Watch your step. Plan ahead. Avoiding accidents before they happen is the best recipe for a rewarding and relaxing hike.

- Ask questions. Forest employees are there to help. It's a lot easier to gain advice beforehand and avoid a mishap away from civilization when it's too late to amend an error. Use your head out there and treat the place as if it were your own backyard. After all, it is your national forest.

Tips for Enjoying Monongahela National Forest

Before you go, call the national forest for an information kit (phone (304) 636-1800). This will help you get oriented to Monongahela's roads, features, and attractions. Detailed maps of the specific wilderness and backcountry areas are available from district ranger stations (see "Contact Information" at the end of this book). They will really help you get around the forest's backcountry. In addition, the following tips will make your visit enjoyable and more rewarding.

- Get out of your car and onto a trail. Auto touring allows a cursory overview of the park—and only from a visual perspective. On the trail you can use your ears and nose as well. This guidebook recommends some trails over others, but any trail is better than no trail at all.

- Investigate different areas of the forest. The Allegheny Trail links the national forest districts. The Cranberry area has thick spruce woods and trout-laden mountain streams. The Spruce Knob-Laurel Fork area offers lesser traveled trails over many locations. The Dolly Sods-Otter Creek area features vast meadows and panoramic views. A mosaic of forest types cover the entirety of the Monongahela. You'll be pleasantly surprised to see so many distinct landscapes in one national forest.

- Take your time along the trails. Pace yourself. The Monongahela is filled with wonders both big and small. Don't rush past a tiny salamander to get to that overlook. Stop and smell the wildflowers. Peer into a clear mountain stream for brook trout. Don't miss the trees for the forest.

- We can't always schedule our free time when we want, but try to hike during the week and avoid the traditional holidays if possible. Trails that are packed in the summer are often clear during the colder months. If you are hiking on a busy day, go early in the morning; it'll enhance your chances of seeing wildlife. The trails really clear out during rainy times, however, don't hike during a thunderstorm.

Backcountry Advice

A permit is not required before entering the backcountry to camp. However, you should practice low-impact camping. Adhere to the adages "Pack it in, pack it out," and "Take only pictures, leave only footprints." Practice "Leave no trace" camping ethics while in the backcountry.

Open fires are permitted except during dry times when the forest service may issue a fire ban. Backpacking stoves are strongly encouraged. You are required to hang your food from bears and other animals in order to minimize human impact on wildlife, avoid their introduction to and dependence on human food. Wildlife learns to associate backpacks and backpackers with easy food sources, thereby influencing their behavior. Make sure you have about 40 feet of thin but sturdy rope to properly secure your food. Ideally, you should throw your rope over a stout limb that extends 10 or more feet above ground. Make sure the rope hangs at least five feet away from the tree trunk.

Solid human waste must be buried in a hole at least three inches deep and at least 200 feet away from trails and water sources; a trowel is basic backpacking equipment.

Following the above guidelines will increase your chances for a pleasant, safe and low-impact interaction between humans and nature. The suggestions are intended to enhance your experience within the confines of this national forest for the flora and fauna of the Allegheny Mountains. Forest regulations can change over time; contact forest ranger stations to confirm the status of any regulations before you enter the backcountry.

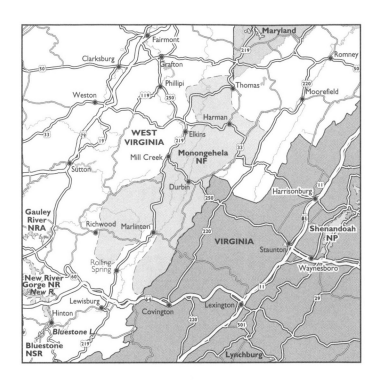

Part I:
There and Back

▲▲▲

Dolly Sods–Otter Creek

Blackbird Knob

Scenery: ★★★★★   Difficulty: ★
Trail Condition: ★★★   Solitude: ★★★
Children: ★★★
Distance: 4.6 miles round-trip
Hiking Time: 2:45 round-trip
Outstanding Features: numerous views,
  varied landscapes

This hike passes through the Dolly Sods Scenic Area, which adjoins the Dolly Sods Wilderness. This whole plateau of spruce forests, rock outcrops, clear streams and open fields is the Monongahela's treasure. The Blackbird Knob Trail gives a good overview of what the Dolly Sods are like. The elevation changes only slightly, so you can concentrate on the view at hand rather than hanging your head sucking wind.

Leave Forest Service Road 75 at the information signs and immediately cross a wet area on elevated wooden planks. Begin climbing through a high country birch, maple, serviceberry forest, that has a stunted look. This forest changes to spruce with occasional open areas. Off to your right at mile 0.2 lies a planted grove of red pine, which is not native to the area.

Beyond here, the trail opens onto a rocky area with great views at mile 0.4. To your left is an open plain and forested ridge forming a bowl around you. Continue to descend in a mostly open area with cherry trees scattered about, and come to Alder Creek at mile 1.1. Just before the creek on your right are old

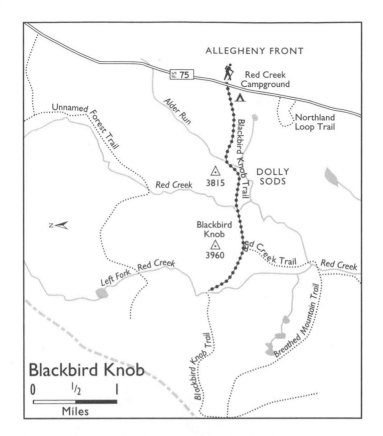

Blackbird Knob

0   ½   1
Miles

beaver dams which have now melded into the clearing and look like waves on the land.

Rock-hop Alder Creek and enter a thick forest for a short distance. The rocky trail soon opens up with views to your left. Enter a cool, dark spruce forest just before coming to Red Creek at mile 1.6. The trail seemingly ends on a small creekside bluff. Turn upstream and rock hop over the stream to the grassy area across the water. Parallel Red Creek upstream for 75 yards, then make a sharp left uphill and away from the water.

Open into a wide plain at mile 1.8, with good views all around. Past the plain, the Blackbird Knob Trail enters a beech forest, coming to a junction with the Red Creek Trail at mile 2.1, with a trail sign which says 2 miles back to Red Creek Campground. Continue forward through this junction, coming to a clearing at mile 2.2. Uphill to your right is a boulder-strewn field. Climb off the footpath and pick your favorite seat in the grandstand. The field is more level farther on. You can see the gorge of Red Creek, with the Alleghenies forming a wall beyond that. Mountain views envelop this side of Blackbird Knob.

Directions: From Petersburg, drive south on West Virginia 28 for 8.5 miles to Jordan Run Road (CR 28/7). Turn right on Jordan Run Road and follow it for 1 mile to Forest Service Road 19, which will be on your left. Turn left on FS 19 and follow it for 6 miles to FS 75. Turn right on FS 75 and follow it for 5 miles to Red Run Campground. The trailhead is just past the campground on your left.

Canyon Rim Trail

Scenery: ★★★★★   Difficulty: ★★
Trail Condition: ★★★★   Solitude: ★★★★
Children: ★★★
Distance: 5.0 miles round-trip
Hiking Time: 3:30 round-trip
Outstanding Features: great views of Blackwater
   Canyon, solitude

Usually to reach a vista, you have to climb to get there. However, this hike actually leads down to its view. Of course, you'll have to climb back to your point of origin. The elevation variations aren't extreme. This hike starts near Olson Lookout Tower. Before you hit the trail, drive 0.3 mile past the trailhead and climb this structure for a view of the northern Monongahela and its surroundings. The view on your hike is of the Blackwater Canyon, reached by the lesser-used Canyon Rim Trail.

Start your hike on the Canyon Rim Trail by leaving the forest road and descending on a raised footbed of soil and stones kept in place by logs. Rhododendron lines the path. Head southeast, dipping and leveling off, then dipping again. Pick up an old railroad grade at 0.7 mile and turn right. Stay with the yellow blazes.

Come to the edge of the canyon at 1.3 miles. The old Flat Rock Trail dips down to your right and dives

Canyon Rim Trail

0   1/2   1

Miles

into the canyon. The Canyon Rim Trail veers left and drops steeply for 0.3 mile. Level off, and turn left again. At mile 1.8, cross a rock and sand streambed, that may or may not have water flowing in it. Begin to look on your right for a footpath leading to an outcrop. This path is about 200 yards beyond the streambed near a spruce tree. It leads down and right to a boulder jumble and a great view of Blackwater Canyon.

Return to the main trail and swing northeasterly along the canyon's rim. Rocks line the old railroad grade. Look in the rhododendron and woods to your left for big rock bluffs. Come to the second viewing area at mile 2.4. This path leads 20 feet to your right onto a relatively flat rock, with views into Big Run and Blackwater Canyon. This vista is easy to miss.

Come to a perennial stream 0.1 mile past this lookout, at mile 2.5. A little bridge of natural stone spans the stream. This is a pretty setting and a water source, but if you come to this stream you have passed the second vista. Backtrack, looking carefully for the little path leading to the second overlook. These views are worth a 500-foot climb back to the car.

Directions: From downtown Davis, drive north on West Virginia 32 for 3 miles to the hamlet of Thomas and US 219. Turn left on US 219, and follow it south for 6.4 miles to Forest Service Road 18. Turn left on FS 18 and follow it 0.4 mile to FS 717, which is dead ahead (FS 18 turns left). Follow FS 717 for 1.3 miles. Canyon Rim Trail will be on your left. The Olson Lookout Tower is 0.3 mile beyond the Canyon Rim Trail.

Chimney Top

Scenery: ★★★★★   Difficulty: ★★★
Trail Condition: ★★★★   Solitude: ★★★
Children: ★★
Distance: 5.8 miles round-trip
Hiking Time: 3:45 round-trip
Outstanding Features: 360° views, history,
   bird life

This is one of the best, and most interesting day hikes in West Virginia. Pass by an old homesite, and while on your way to great views, maybe you'll be lucky enough to see a peregrine falcon, which nest on the rocky west side of North Fork Mountain. But like most hikes with a view, you have to do a little climbing to get there. Gain 1,700 feet on the way. Be apprised: there is no water on this trail.

Your hike is on the North Fork Mountain Trail (Forest Trail No. 501). Immediately climb a small hill, then pass by an old homesite on your left. The level area is growing up in forest. Notice the rocks piles on the vicinity hillsides; this indicates once-tilled land. Briefly connect to an old woods road heading back to the homesite, then begin a steady rise through a hickory-oak woodland growing over the rocky soil.

At 0.5 mile the trail swings left onto a piney point of a ridge. Mountain laurel grows in abundance beneath the conifers. Enjoy the level stretch, then climb around the heads of some dry coves before coming to another point of a ridge at mile 1.0. More switchbacks take you up the side of North Fork Mountain. There are obscured views back to the

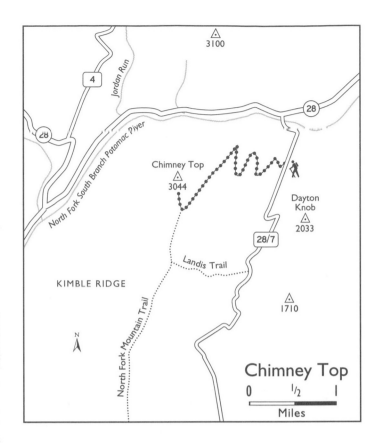

Chimney Top

0   1/2   1

Miles

north of Petersburg. Come to your first outcrop at mile 1.9. This is the beginning of the escarpment that runs along the west side of the mountain for some distance. Look to your left and you can see the wall of stone rising up the mountain. Notice the abundance of Virginia pine atop the ridge.

Make a southerly track along the ridge, paralleling the escarpment. Grand views lie to your right just a few steps away. The ridge rises well above the trail. Begin to look for a pile of white rocks on either side of the trail, which are at mile 2.8. They mark the side trail to the Chimney Top that comes in at an acute angle on your right. If you come to a grassy area with many dead trees, you have gone too far. Either way, head right up to the nearly continual rock outcrop atop the ridge. The actual Chimney Rock is the highest one you see, and takes a little climbing. Be careful, there is sand on the rocks here. A USGS Survey Marker lies atop the rock at mile 2.9. Below is the

North Fork and across from that is the high plateau of Dolly Sods. To your south is the long escarpment and the rest of North Fork Mountain fading in the distance. Keep your eye on the sky for falcons riding the thermals around you.

Directions: From Petersburg, drive 6.8 miles south on West Virginia 28 to County Road 28/11. Look for the sign for Smoke Hole Recreation Area and Big Bend Campground. Immediately cross the North Fork Potomac River, then continue up the gravel road for 0.3 mile. The signed North Fork Mountain Trail will be on your right.

Red Creek Plains

Scenery: ★★★★★   Difficulty: ★
Trail Condition: ★★★★   Solitude: ★★
Children: ★★★★
Distance: 3.6 miles round-trip
Hiking Time: 2:45 round-trip
Outstanding Features: good views, high altitude bogs, heath glades

This hike traverses the Red Creek Plains, a mostly forested area of high altitude wetlands, rock outcrops, and spruce forests. The trail over the plains, South Prong, has been improved, making a rewarding trek for hikers of all ages. Once, this area was completely forested. Following logging, what was left of the woods was burned down to bedrock. It has taken several decades for the forest to return. Still, there remains great views and attractive environments such as open bogs of moss, tundra flora, and heath glades, which are low-lying plant communities of mountain laurel, azalea and blueberry.

Start your hike on the upper South Prong Trail on a boardwalk that crosses and preserves a wet bog below you. This is the first of 12 such boardwalks that are installed on the first 0.8 mile of path, extending from 10 feet to 100 feet in length. These raised bridges allow water to pass naturally under you, instead of

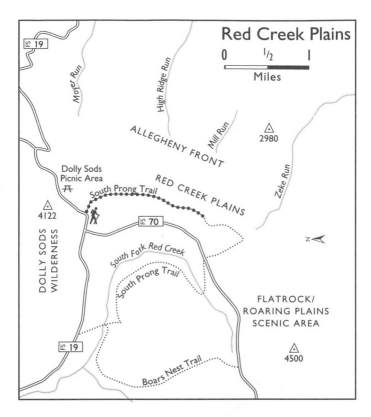

being dammed by a grooved trail. Much of this initial section is also graveled, making for easier passage and better drainage.

Between these numerous wet clearings are stands of spruce and small meadows, and the canopy opens overhead more often than not. Pass through a boulder field at 0.7 mile, and top out on a rock flat at mile 1.2. From the rock flat, there is nothing but spruce around you. There are good views of the wooded Flatrock Plains to the east and South Fork Red Creek valley to your west. Descend between some large, dark boulders into a thick spruce wood. The trail continues to alternate environments rapidly, including some northern red oak trees that grow low and wide in response to harsh conditions.

Make the only significant climb of the hike at mile 1.7. And this one is short. Once you top out, look for a small trail leading to your right. Walk about 50 feet to a boulder field. This is your Red Plains grandstand. The view opens up to your north and east. South Fork

Red Creek is below you, and the Dolly Sods lie in the northern distance. To your east are the mountains beyond the Allegheny Front.

Directions: From Petersburg, drive south on West Virginia 28 for 8.5 miles to Jordan Run Road (CR 28/7). Turn right on Jordan Run Road and follow it for 1 mile to Forest Service Road 19, which will be on your left. Turn left on FS 19 and follow it for 6 miles to FS 75. Turn left on FS 75 and follow it for 1 mile to the upper South Prong trailhead, which will be on your left.

Rohrbaugh Overlook

Scenery: ★★★★★   Difficulty: ★★
Trail Condition: ★★★★   Solitude: ★★
Children: ★★★★
Distance: 3.6 miles round-trip
Hiking Time: 3:00 round-trip
Outstanding Features: best views in Dolly Sods
  Wilderness backcountry

This hike follows an old forest service road down to the rim of Red Creek Canyon. From there it parallels the rim to an overlook on a huge outcrop that avails views of the heart of the Dolly Sods Wilderness. The downgrade from the trailhead is moderate but steady. Others will be heading down to this view. Start your hike on the Wildlife Trail, so-named because it was used by the forest service in pre-wilderness days to access grassy food plots for game. These clearings are still along the pathway. Enter a deciduous forest and immediately pick up the old forest road, turning left and passing a trailside information board. Behind this board is the first former wildlife clearing. The woods around you are dominated by beech trees.

Ease down toward the Red Creek valley, making a wide switchback to the right at 0.4 mile. Step over a streamlet and pass a big meadow. This trail traces a linear clearing that is irregularly canopied. The forest will eventually take over here. Parallel the stream you

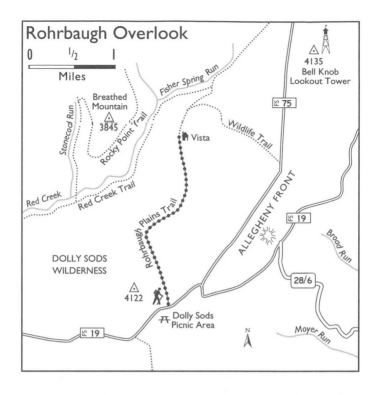

Rohrbaugh Overlook

0   ½   1
Miles

Fisher Spring Run

Breathed
Mountain
△
3845

Stonecoal Run

Rocky Point Trail

4135
Bell Knob
Lookout Tower

🗲 75

Wildlife Trail

🏠 Vista

Red Creek

Red Creek Trail

Rohrbaugh Plains Trail

ALLEGHENY FRONT

🗲 19

Broad Run

DOLLY SODS
WILDERNESS

△
4122

🧍

28/6

🍴 Dolly Sods
Picnic Area

🗲 19

N
🡇

Moyer Run

just crossed. Cross the stream again at mile 1.0 and skirt the upper edge of a meadow. Reenter the woods and come to a trail junction at mile 1.2. This is the Rohrbaugh Plains Trail. To your right the path drops off into Red Creek. You, however, follow the Rohrbaugh Plains Trail forward, staying with the roadbed. Ascend slightly along the edge of the Red Creek canyon. Cruise through another large meadow, and pass a couple of trails leading right to small outcrops with some views. These don't compare to what lies ahead. Pass an often dry streambed and come to a small clearing with more outcrops to your right.

Keep going, then come to some massive white rock cliffs on your right at mile 1.8. Walk out here and take in the view. Just across are the cliffs of Breathed Mountain. Below you and to the left is the lower Red Creek valley. To the far left are more cliffs along the Rohrbaugh Plains trail. To your right is the upper Red Creek valley. This is one of the best vistas in the entire Monongahela National Forest.

Directions: From Petersburg, drive south on West Virginia Road 28 for 8.5 miles to Jordan Run Road (CR 28/7). Turn right on Jordan Run Road and follow it for 1 mile to Forest Service Road 19, which will be on your left. Turn left on FS 19 and follow it for 6 miles to FS 75. Turn right on FS 75 and follow it for 1.5 miles to the Wildlife Trail parking area, which will be on your left.

Seneca Rocks

Scenery: ★★★★★   Difficulty: ★★
Trail Condition: ★★★★   Solitude: ★
Children: ★★★★
Distance: 2.6 miles round-trip
Hiking Time: 2:00 round-trip
Outstanding Features: views, interesting geology

Landmarks, by definition, stand out. However, some landmarks stand out more than others. The Seneca Rocks are one of West Virginia's most outstanding landmarks. These outcrops tower nearly 900 feet above the valley of the North Fork of the South Branch Potomac River. The pinnacles are very popular with rock climbers. We hikers are forced to enjoy the foot trail to a viewing platform, where the views are merely stunning, without the risk associated with rock climbing. There will be others enjoying this trail with you—many won't make it to the top, even though it is only 1.3 miles to the viewing platform, and the trail is well-graded with many benches available for resting. Hike this trail in the morning if possible—it's shady and cooler then.

Start your hike near the Seneca Rocks Discovery Center, heading toward the North Fork of the South Branch Potomac River. Walk a very wide gravel footpath. Seneca Rocks are right in front of you above the treeline. Come to a wide, long, and elaborate pedestrian bridge over the river. The gravel footpath continues. Notice the trailside interpretive displays designed to enhance your appreciation of the area. The trail soon splits. Rock climbers go right; hikers stay left.

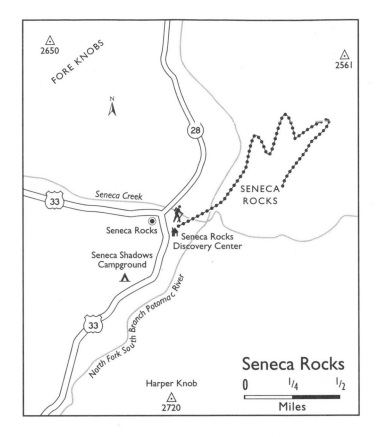

Notice the trail has been cleared of boulders that otherwise litter the hickory-oak forest. These rocks have fallen over time from the Seneca Rocks above. Wooden fences line the trail to discourage switchbacking. The climbing begins in earnest at 0.3 mile as the trail gains elevation via a series of steps. Next come many switchbacks, as the pathway rises as gradually as possible despite the very steep terrain. Signs mark 1/4 of the way and 1/2 of the way.

The Seneca Rocks are out of view as you switchback up the mountainside. Keep on climbing, coming to a final series of steps, then reach the viewing platform at mile 1.3. From the platform you can see way down from where you came and beyond. A display shows you exactly what lies in the distance. Beyond the platform is a rock promontory with good views in all directions. Be very careful if you go this route. The drop-offs are sheer and are recommended for rock climbers only. Do not walk one step beyond your capabilities. After looking out, you'll appreciate the walk back down.

Directions: From the town of Seneca Rocks, drive north on State Road 55/28 for 100 yards to the Seneca Rocks Discovery Center. The trail starts by the river near the restored log house.

Table Rock

Scenery: ★★★★★   Difficulty: ★
Trail Condition: ★★★   Solitude: ★★★
Children: ★★★★
Distance: 2.4 miles round-trip
Hiking Time: 1:45 round-trip
Outstanding Features: massive rock outcrop with
  great views

This is a very moderate hike with a great reward. The Table Rock Trail, Forest Trail No. 113, leads to the craggy western edge of Canaan Mountain, a high elevation plateau featuring a flora more like Canada than West Virginia. Be forewarned that the trail is muddy in spots and Table Rock outcrop has some big crevasses, so keep the kids close at bay while taking in the great view of the Dry Fork and Cheat River valleys. This trail is part of the Canaan (pronounced: ka-nane) Mountain Backcountry Area in the Potomac Highlands near Dolly Sods. This area receives light hiking pressure, due to not being designated an official wilderness.

Start your hike from Canaan Loop Road and enter the northern hardwood forest of beech, black cherry, maple and yellow birch. The blue diamond marked trail is nearly level, then slabs the side of a hill on your left, then soon levels again. Below you lie mosses, ferns, and a lot of rocks.

At 0.6 mile the trail descends a bit, then levels out in a rhododendron thicket that is muddy in spots. The trail then turns a little more southwesterly as you pick your way along the muck. Try to stay on the trail—if

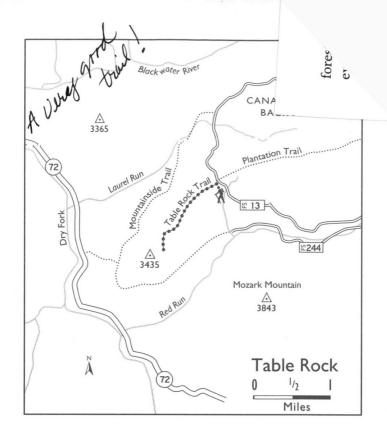

you walk on the edge of the wet area, the wet area will only widen. In many areas, branches and other pieces of wood have been thrown down as dry spots on which to set your feet.

Come to a campsite just before reaching Table Rock, where the trail splits. The primary trail goes left to an outcrop. Here, the large level rock face opens to the Dry Fork gorge below. Watch for the crevasses in the rock on which you are standing. Also notice the mountain laurel and small spruce clinging to the thin soils atop Table Rock. Across from you lies Green Mountain. A spruce forest resides atop Green Mountain and is surrounded by hardwoods. Return to the campsite, and this time go to the right for a better view into the Cheat River Valley and the mountains beyond.

As you work your way around the outcrops, you'll notice how some of these ledges overhang. Look down from Table Rock and see how some boulders couldn't stand the test of time and have fallen to the

below. Some of the crevasses on this side are
en deeper—100 feet or more. Watch your footing,
find a good spot, and take it all in.

Directions: From the town of Davis, drive south on
State Road 32 for 3.3 miles to Canaan Loop Road. Turn
right on Canaan Loop Road and follow it for 10 miles
to the Table Rock Trail, which will be on your left.

Upper Red Creek

Scenery: ★★★★★   Difficulty: ★★
Trail Condition: ★★★★   Solitude: ★★★
Children: ★★★
Distance: 5.8 miles round-trip
Hiking Time: 3:45 round-trip
Outstanding Features: extraordinary vistas from grass
  plains

This hike cruises through the northern portion of the
Dolly Sods Scenic Area. There are nearly continuous
great views of the upper Red Creek drainage and surroundings as you walk through meadows and scattered woodlands to the confluence of Red Creek and
an unnamed stream that flows off Raven Ridge. The
net elevation change is only a little more than 200
feet, making an easy hike. This portion of Dolly Sods
was purchased by the forest service in the early 1990s.
An official trail system has not been developed yet, so
this trail currently has no name or number. But it is
very easy to follow using old Jeep roads.

The high plateau here was used as a bombing
range during World War II, so theoretically you could
encounter an unexploded munition. If so, do not
touch it! Draw a map of the area and report it to the
forest service in Petersburg. However, this risk is very
slight. The area around the trailhead is very open.
Step around the roadside boulders and begin
descending slightly through a heath glade of low-
lying blueberry, azalea, and mountain laurel. Notice
how the plants are bent to the east and stunted. Life
can be harsh up here. Ahead and to your left is the

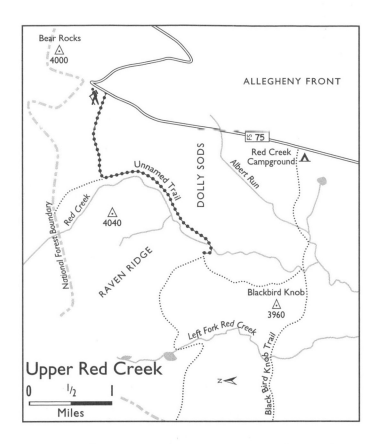

Upper Red Creek

0   ¹/₂   1
Miles

shallow valley of Red Creek. To your right are high meadows broken with stunted spruce trees.

Drop down to a tributary of Red Creek at 0.5 mile. Climb out of the streambed through a deciduous forest, passing a huge boulder in the middle of the trail before topping out on a hill with extraordinary views to the south. Descend again toward Red Creek, coming to a trail junction at 1.1 miles, marked with a rock cairn. Turn left on the old Jeep road and head down the valley of Red Creek. Around you are meadows and scattered woods and more views. Aspen trees line the trail in spots.

Work your way around wet areas and a beaver dam, then come to another junction at mile 1.7. Stay right with the Jeep road, traversing a rocky area. The walking then becomes easy on an old railroad grade as the meadow opens wide, with trees few and far between. Come to Red Creek at mile 2.7. Step over the stream, and angle for the hill up to your right. This is your destination and viewing spot. There are great views in nearly all directions, and a tree or two for shade. This view will make you appreciate the forest service land purchase of the 1990s.

Directions: From Petersburg, drive south on West Virginia 28 for 8.5 miles to Jordan Run Road (CR 28/7). Turn right on Jordan Run Road and follow it for 1.0 mile to Forest Service Road 19, which will be on your left. Turn left on FS 19 and follow it for 6.0 miles to FS 75. Turn right on FS 75 and follow it for 7.2 miles to a trailhead on your left that is blocked with white boulders lining the road and has a "Foot Travel Welcome" sign. You have gone too far if you make a hairpin turn to the right and begin dropping off the plateau. Backtrack 0.2 mile to the trailhead.

Spruce Knob-Laurel Fork Area

East Fork Greenbrier

Scenery: ★★★★   Difficulty: ★★
Trail Condition: ★★★★   Solitude: ★★★★
Children: ★★★
Distance: 8.0 miles round-trip
Hiking Time: 4:30 round-trip
Outstanding Features: intimate river valley, small waterfall

This hike takes you along the headwaters of one of West Virginia's most famed rivers — the Greenbrier. Walk alongside the East Fork of Greenbrier River through forests, meadows, and plantings of red spruce to a small waterfall. This valley hike can be done any time of year, since it stays on the right bank of the stream its entire length using old roads, grades, and trails, and thus has no fords. Spring and fall are especially attractive times to hike this path.

Leave the Island Campground near the restrooms. Begin heading north up the river valley on a grade

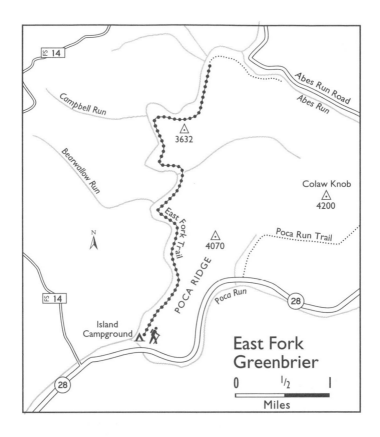

beneath a deciduous forest with pockets of hemlock. Swing around a mucky spot in the path, then come alongside East Fork at 0.4 mile. This clear headwater stream holds wary trout that scatter upon your passing. At 0.7 mile, the trail veers up Poca Ridge to your right, leaving the East Fork flood plain, avoiding a possible ford. Soon, drop back down and hug the right edge of the river valley through an open grassy area, regaining the old grade. At mile 1.1, leave the river bottom again, scurrying up the ridgeside. Up here, intersect an old trail coming in from your right. There are nice, elevated views of the East Fork from here.

Drop back down to the river and open into a big meadow at mile 1.4. Look at the surrounding ridges, and stay on the right edge of the meadow. Toward the end of the clearing, as the stream curves to the right, watch for the trail curving up the hillside to your right, at the old roadbed. Swing around the curve in the stream, then climb up Poca Ridge on a smaller trail. It levels out a couple hundred feet above East Fork, and meanders along the ridge.

Pass a side stream coming in from your right at mile 2.0, and drop once again to the East Fork. The streamside flat is mostly covered in trees, with some open areas grown up with ferns, which turn gold in early fall. Look for signs of beaver activity here. At mile 2.3, toward the end of the flat, the trail again jogs right onto the hillside. Work along the ridge and drop to the valley floor at mile 2.7, ending up in a streamside spruce thicket.

The evergreen-planted flat ends at mile 3.1, as the watercourse and hillside pinch in the trail. Once again, the trail climbs away from the flood plain into a woodland of yellow birch. Achieve the river bottom at mile 3.6, but, as the pattern goes, climb once again up the ridgeside, then drop down into another spruce thicket.

Continue upstream, looking toward the East Fork. Just as you leave the river bottom, there is a waterfall off to your left on the East Fork. Head toward the river and your destination. At mile 4.0, the East Fork forms a horseshoe, dropping a few feet into a deep pool suitable for swimming. There is a small grassy area by the falls, ideal for relaxing.

Directions: From the town of Bartow at the intersection of US 250 and WV 28/92, drive south on US 250 for 2.2 miles. Veer left, staying on WV 28 for 2.6 more miles (US 250 veers right) and Island Campground will be on your left.

High Falls

Scenery: ★★★★★	Difficulty: ★★★★
Trail Condition: ★★★	Solitude: ★★★
Children: ★	

Distance: 8.2 miles round-trip
Hiking Time: 5:15 round-trip
Outstanding Features: best waterfall in the
  Monongahela

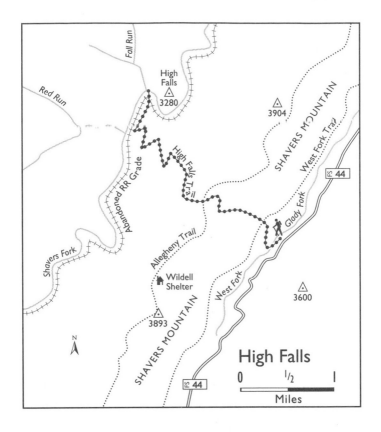

High Falls

0   1/2   1

Miles

On this hike, you are well-rewarded for your efforts. Leave the West Fork Glady Creek valley and steeply climb up Shavers Mountain, then drop down Shavers Mountain on a series of switchbacks to Shavers Fork. Here, follow a defunct railroad track downstream along Shavers Fork to the High Falls of Cheat, a wide falls that is very scenic, and one of my favorite falls in West Virginia.

Leave Forest Service Road 44 on the High Falls Trail and drop down to an old roadbed. Turn left to parallel FS 44, then veer right at 0.1 mile, entering a partially wooded meadow. Cross West Fork Glady creek at 0.2 mile, then pass through a wood gate. Wind through more meadows broken with hawthorn trees, and come to the West Fork Trail at 0.5 mile, where wooden fences line either side of the trail. Stay forward on the High Falls Trail, ascending through an open meadow to briefly reenter the woods, then traverse a final clearing.

Begin to switchback up the side of Shavers Mountain, passing another old fence at 0.8 mile. Keep climbing through maple-beech woods, crossing a logging road at mile 1.4. A few years back, this road was used to timber the nearby clearings, and the trailbed became rocky. Continue ascending to arrive at a gap, then a trail junction at mile 1.9. To your left and right the Allegheny Trail runs the crest of Shavers Mountain. Keep forward on the High Falls Trail, marked with blue diamonds.

Swing through an evergreen forest and intersect a grassy lane at mile 2.1. Turn right and follow the road 0.2 mile. Then dive left into the woods at a signed turn. Just below here the trail has been rerouted. Instead of dropping steeply down to Shavers Fork, the High Falls Trail turns right and crosses a streambed, then heads north, descending via several switchbacks onto a rock-lined footpath. Pass through a rock field at mile 3.0.

The waters of Shavers Fork soon become audible. The final switchback is to the left. Briefly pick up an old railroad grade, then turn sharply right down to the old railroad, arriving at mile 3.4. The ties and tracks still remain, although the track is inactive. Turn right on the railroad tracks and follow them downstream. Walking the tracks is eerie at first — at times it seems as if a train is going to come around the bend. There are good views of Cheat Mountain to your left.

After a long 0.7 mile of track walking, the rail makes a sharp turn to the right. Look for a pile of rocks in a grassy area to your left. The High Falls of Cheat are clearly audible. Take the trail straight down to the river, passing a couple of campsites. Come out on top of the falls at mile 4.1. Shavers Fork curves in a horseshoe of over 100 feet and drops down about 20 feet. Take a footpath through the rhododendron to enjoy the falls from below. There is a deep hole down here for swimming.

Directions: From Elkins, drive east on US 33 for 12.6 miles over Alpena Gap to the hamlet of Alpena. Turn right on Glady Road, County Road 27 (just across from the Alpine Motel). Follow Glady Road for 9.2 miles to Glady. Turn left on Middle Mountain Road, CR 22, and follow it for 0.2 mile to Glady-Durbin Road, Forest Service Road 44. Turn right on FS 44, which soon turns to gravel. Keep on FS 44 for 3.9 miles to the High Falls Trail, which starts on your right.

Huckleberry Trail

Scenery: ★★★★   Difficulty: ★★
Trail Condition: ★★★★   Solitude: ★★
Children: ★★★
Distance: 4.0 miles round-trip
Hiking Time: 2:45 round-trip
Outstanding Features: high ridge, good views

This hike takes you along a portion of the highest ridge in West Virginia. Follow the Huckleberry Trail north along Spruce Mountain, meandering through boulder fields, spruce woods, and low-slung heath meadows to a viewpoint from a rock outcrop. While up here, also

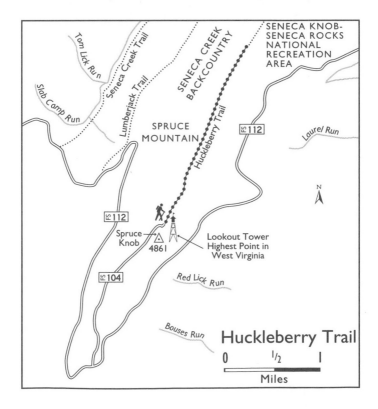

Huckleberry Trail

0   ¹/₂   1

Miles

take the short walk to the Spruce Knob Observation Tower, which is West Virginia's highest point. This whole area exudes a high country aura.

First, walk the wide trail to the observation tower, and then make this trek to your own observation point on Spruce Mountain, which is a north-south linear ridge. Take the Huckleberry Trail, which enters a forest of stunted spruce trees and brush. The canopy is mostly open above the rocky path. At 0.2 mile, swing around a boulder field and look to your left for a side trail leading left to an outcrop with views west.

The trail bed becomes surprisingly sandy in spots. Alternate between dark, shady spruce thickets and more open brushy areas. Make a brief descent at 0.8 mile. The woods become more thickly canopied. Level out and begin a moderate upgrade, where forest and meadow alternate.

At mile 1.9, in a clearing, pass an upright stone marker that has "2 MI" carved onto it. Shortly past this stone marker, look for a footpath leading left. Take this side trail for approximately 100 yards to a boulder field. There are good views of the Seneca Creek backcountry to your north and west. This view may not be as good as that from the observation tower, but it is more well-earned.

Directions: From the town of Seneca Rocks, head south on US 33 for 13 miles to Briery Gap Road. Turn right on Briery Gap Road and follow it for 2.5 miles to Forest Service Road 112. Turn right on FS 112 and head up 7.3 miles to FS 104. Turn right onto FS 104 and follow it for 2.0 miles to the Spruce Knob parking area. The Huckleberry Trail starts on the north side of the parking area, opposite the trail to the Spruce Knob Observation Tower.

Laurel Fork Wilderness North

Scenery: ★★★★   Difficulty: ★★
Trail Condition: ★★★   Solitude: ★★★★
Children: ★★★
Distance: 8.0 miles round-trip
Hiking Time: 5:00 round-trip
Outstanding Features: wilderness character with
   meadows and views

This hike takes you deep into the heart of the lower Laurel Fork Valley. There are views down here of Middle Mountain and valley meadows, where Laurel Fork breaks up into numerous runs encircling large islands. This is good deer country—you may see a doe or two among the hills, hollows, and stream meanders. The Laurel River Trail follows old railroad grades and railbeds, and is fairly easy to follow. However, this is

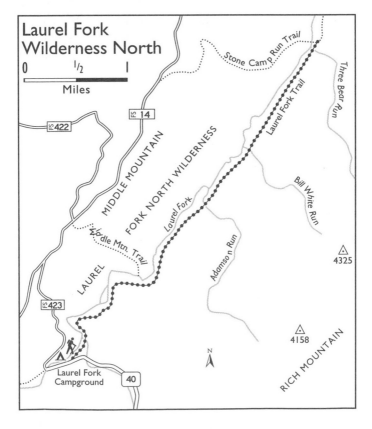

a federally designated wilderness; there are no trail signs or arrows or blazes to mark your route. On the other hand, there are no major stream crossings, and the relatively low elevation makes this a good hike for spring or autumn.

Leave the area of forest service buildings at Laurel Fork Campground, and cross the wooden bridge over Laurel Fork. Walk through the lower loop of the campground and pick up the Laurel River Trail, which leaves at the northern end of the loop near an information kiosk. The trail heads into the woods and immediately bears left to pick up an old elevated railbed. Be on the lookout for the numerous errant paths in the area.

Laurel Fork is off to your left. Cross a couple of small streambeds while walking beneath a hardwood forest of cherry, yellow birch, and occasional hemlocks. Emerge onto a field after the second streambed at 0.2 mile. Another path merges in from your right; stay forward and cross Lick Run at the far end of the field. The trail then becomes pinched in by Laurel Fork on your left and a steep hillside to your right. There is a deep pool in the stream here and good views of Laurel Fork and the mountains beyond.

At 0.6 mile, Laurel River Trail bends right with the creek, comes to a field, then diverges uphill from the river on a road bed. Climb away from the stream— the walking is pleasant through the open forest. Pass through a dark hemlock thicket at mile 1.1. Drop down and return to Laurel Fork at mile 1.7. The Middle Mountain Trail merges in from across Laurel Fork, but is very hard to find. You stay forward on the easy-to-trace Laurel River. There is a large broken meadow across the way.

Enter streamside hemlock thicket at mile 2.1. Ahead, the grade splits—veer left into a clearing and cross Adamson Run. Stay right across the field and pick up the railbed once again. At mile 2.5 there is a tunnel of hemlock that makes day seem like dusk. Beyond this, field and forest interplay, and in clearings, Middle Mountain is in view off to your left. At mile 3.0, step over Bill White Run, and immediately climb right, into a small clearing. Stay forward and drop back down to the creek at mile 3.3. Keep heading downstream and pass Shine Hollow at mile 3.5. Here, a streambed descends steeply from your right.

A massive meadow opens to your left as the valley floor widens. The trail leaves the woods and enters a clearing at mile 4.0. Immediately cross Three Bear Run in the clearing. Just a bit farther in the field, the trail comes to an unmarked junction. To your left, the Stone Camp Run Trail crosses Laurel Fork and heads up Middle Mountain. The Laurel River Trail veers right, renters the woods, and picks up another grade continuing downstream. This is your destination. You can rest in the meadow or in the woods of Three Bear Run. There are also some nice pools just downstream in Laurel Fork. Relax and take in some wilderness before heading back.

Directions: From Elkins, drive east on US 33 for 12.6 miles over Alpena Gap to the hamlet of Alpena. Turn right on Glady Road, County Road 27 (just across from the Alpine Motel). Follow Glady Road for 9.2 miles to Glady. Turn left on Middle Mountain Road (Forest Service Road 422) and drive for 4.6 miles to FS 14. Turn right, on FS 14 and drive south for 0.3 miles to FS 423. Turn left on FS 423 and drive 1.5 miles to Laurel Fork Campground. Park near the forest service buildings along FS 423.

Laurel Fork Wilderness South

Scenery: ★★★★   Difficulty: ★★★
Trail Condition: ★★   Solitude: ★★★★★
Children: ★★
Distance: 8.6 miles round-trip
Hiking Time: 5:15 round-trip
Outstanding Features: meadows, attractive hardwood forest, wilderness setting

This there and back hike deserves two trips. The hardwood forests, often carpeted in a fern understory,

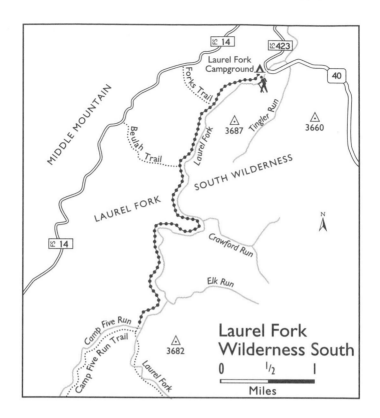

Laurel Fork Wilderness South

0   ¹/₂   1

Miles

are outstanding. They are punctuated by numerous meadows, and through it all flows Laurel Fork, a mountain trout stream worthy of federal wilderness designation. Take the Laurel River Trail upstream along Laurel Fork into a quiet valley. Head up to the confluence of Laurel Fork and Camp Five Run, where there is a meadow for sun worshippers or an evergreen thicket for shade lovers.

Start your hike near the forest buildings of Laurel Fork Campground. Head south past the pump well and upper campground loop, then come to the Laurel River trailhead proper. Enter the woods on an old railroad bed. Pass a spring pipe on your right at 0.2 mile, which was used when the campground was a Civilian Conservation Corps Camp.

Continue up the grade; a meadow and Laurel Fork are off to your left. At 0.6 mile, come to a wooden post indicating the intersection with the Forks Trail, Forest Trail No. 323. Continue forward on the Laurel River

Trail and drop down to skirt the right edge of a meadow, and reenter the woods. There is beaver evidence to your left. Come very near Laurel Fork, then enter a sometimes flooded area shaded with hemlock and yellow birch trees.

At mile 1.2, cross a meander onto an island of Laurel Fork, then soon cross back over to the right bank and clamber up the rocky mountainside. Laurel Fork is now well below you. At mile 1.6, dip into a hollow where there is a small stream, and come to a post indicating the junction with the Beulah Trail, FT No. 310. Stay on the Laurel River Trail, dropping left off the rail bed at mile 2.1. The forest is very attractive here, with the silvery trunks of yellow birch rising above the ferns.

At mile 2.5, the trail swings sharply right around a boulder outcrop. You are far above Laurel Fork. Down below, a huge beaver-created pool is at the Laurel Fork confluence with Crawford Run. Soon drop down toward the forests and fields by the stream, passing through a thicket of young beech trees. Skirt the right edge of a meadow at mile 2.9. Come to a rill flowing in from your right through broken woods at mile 3.1. Step over the water and continue to parallel Laurel Fork. Look for rock cairns to help guide you through this potentially confusing area. The path climbs away from the stream briefly, only to drop down again to a boggy area.

Continue to parallel Laurel Fork, passing very close to the stream. Look for an especially large hemlock beside the watercourse at mile 3.8, then once again swing away from the creek, only to drop down to a railbed. Come to a red pine plantation at mile 4.1, where field and forest mix. Stay with the railbed, and at mile 4.3 watch for a conspicuous pile of rock. Here the trail seemingly splits. To your right, the railbed enters a large meadow beside Camp Five Run. To your left, the Laurel Fork Trail bisects a couple of red spruce, then crosses Camp Five Run and enters a deep dark thicket of hemlock and spruce. In this thicket is the confluence of Laurel Fork and Camp Five Run. If you like sun, head for the field; if you like shade, head for the thicket. Either spot makes for a good destination.

Directions: From Elkins, drive east on US 33 for 12.6 miles over Alpena Gap to the hamlet of Alpena. Turn right on Glady Road, County Road 27 (just across from the Alpine Motel). Follow Glady Road for 9.2 miles to Glady. Turn left on Middle Mountain Road (Forest Service Road 422) and drive for 4.6 miles to FS 14. Turn right on FS 14 and drive south for 0.3 mile to FS 423. Turn left on FS 423 and drive 1.5 miles to Laurel Fork Campground. Park near the forest service buildings along FS 423.

Upper Falls of Seneca

Scenery: ★★★★★   Difficulty: ★★
Trail Condition: ★★★★   Solitude: ★★
Children: ★★
Distance: 9.8 miles round-trip
Hiking Time: 5:15 round-trip
Outstanding Features: many waterfalls, meadows

This hike could be called "Numerous Falls of Seneca," for there are many other cataracts on this hike than the final destination, the actual Upper Falls of Seneca. Other parts of Seneca Creek have cascades, and many tributaries of Seneca Creek have falls of their own. Throw in some meadows and attractive mountain valley scenery and you have one of the finest walks in the Monongahela.

Start your hike by leaving Forest Service Road 112, and following the Seneca Creek Trail down the valley of Seneca Creek. The path is partially canopied by spruce and hardwoods. Step over Trussel Run at 0.4 mile. Just past this is a broken meadow framed by the ridge dividing Randolph and Pendleton counties. Seneca Creek lies off to your left. Intersect the Tom Lick Trail at 0.9 mile, staying forward on the Seneca Creek Trail. The path is sometimes open and sometimes lined with spruce. The valley to your left has many more meadows and occasional beaver dams.

Numerous feeder streams flow in from Spruce Mountain to your right. Cross Beech Run at mile 1.9. Wind through some hardwoods, and pass the Swallow Rock Trail at mile 2.1.

Keep heading down the valley and cross Seneca Creek at mile 2.7. Look for bluffs and waterfalls across the watercourse just before arriving at the Judy Springs Walk-In Campground at mile 3.2. Veer left through a field, shortly passing the Bear Hunter Trail. Bend to the right and look for two more side falls, entering Seneca Creek on the far side of the stream. Make a wet ford of Seneca Creek at mile 3.6. Just past

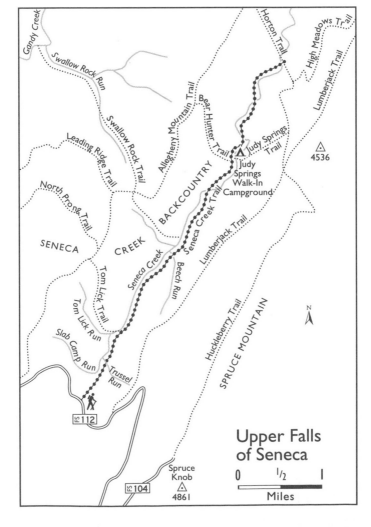

the ford, look for two large falls on Seneca Creek. Make another ford at mile 4.1. Keep down the valley of birch, beech, and maple, looking for other old logging grades on the hillsides.

Come to a meadow at mile 4.6. Look for pair of side falls to your right, before coming to the final ford of Seneca Creek at mile 4.9. Be careful here, as the ford is just above a six-foot cascade. Just ahead is the Huckleberry Trail, leaving to your right. Continue just a bit farther and come to the Upper Falls of Seneca. Here, Seneca Creek drops a good 30 feet into a pool. A trail leads down to the pool, where you can see how narrow the falls are at the top and how they fan out below. Upper Falls of Seneca is the climax of the multitude of cataracts on this hike.

Directions: From the town of Seneca Rocks, head south on US 33 for 13 miles to Briery Gap Road. Turn right on Briery Gap Road and follow it up for 2.5 miles to Forest Service Road 112. Turn right on FS 112 and head up 11.3 miles to the Seneca Creek trailhead, which will be on your right.

Shavers Mountain via Johns Camp Run

Scenery: ★★★★
Trail Condition: ★★★
Children: ★
Distance: 4.8 miles round-trip
Hiking Time: 3:15 round-trip
Outstanding Features: rock scramble, trail shelter, views

Difficulty: ★★★
Solitude: ★★★★

This hike takes you through a lesser traveled area of the national forest. Take the Johns Camp Run Trail to the Allegheny Trail and a shelter used by overnight hikers. Head north on the Allegheny Trail on Shavers Mountain over one knob to another knob and a boulder outcrop, where a rock scramble leads to views of the mountains around you. This rock scramble over massive boulders is not suitable for children. On the

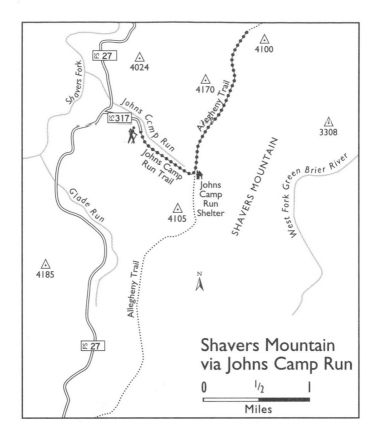

Shavers Mountain
via Johns Camp Run

0   ½   1

Miles

way to the trailhead is the Gaudineer Scenic Area. Stop by here to view an old growth spruce forest.

For the Shavers Mountain hike, leave the parking area on the old Jeep road and pass an earthen vehicle barricade. The grassy path is lined with young spruce, with a northern hardwood forest overhead. The climb is moderate as small streamlets cross the trail. Johns Camp Run is off to your left. Work your way through some mucky areas. At 0.5 mile, the path abruptly leaves the grade right and winds upward through the woods as a foot trail. Step over a spring branch at 0.7 mile and come to Allegheny Trail and a backcountry shelter 0.1 mile farther. Here in a gap, an open-fronted Adirondack shelter is used by overnight campers walking the long-distance Allegheny Trail.

Turn left on the Allegheny Trail, following the yellow blazes north. Climb out of the gap, leveling out at mile 1.2. Soon, come to a patch of red spruce. Here, look on your right for a cleared view of the Greenbrier River valley, Middle Mountain, and the Alleghenies beyond. Continue on the Allegheny Trail, skirting a high point to your left and dropping down to a gap at mile 1.9. Begin to climb up the nose of the ridge to another knob. Level out again. By mile 2.3, the terrain has become littered with boulders.

Here, look for the highest outcrop of boulders off to your right, and begin to climb them to a high point, which is a couple hundred feet distant, and not very obvious from the trail. Be very careful while scrambling, as there are 10- to 15-foot crevasses between some of these cabin-sized boulders. From the highest boulder, view Cheat Mountain to your west. More scrambling around will avail some views back to the east. This rock jumble is a fun place to explore to find more vistas and small rock shelters of your own.

Directions: From the Greenbrier Ranger Station in Bartow, head north on US 250 for 7.5 miles to Forest Service Road 27 and a sign for Gaudineer Scenic Area. Turn right on FS 27 and follow it 4.3 miles to FS 317. Turn right on FS 317 and follow it 0.4 mile to a dead end and the Johns Camp Run trailhead.

Cranberry Area

Big Beechy Run Falls

Scenery: ★★★★   Difficulty: ★
Trail Condition: ★★★★★   Solitude: ★★
Children: ★★★★
Distance: 4.8 miles round-trip
Hiking Time: 3:00 round-trip
Outstanding Features: waterfall, attractive valley

This is a moderate hike to a pretty destination located within the Cranberry Wilderness. Stroll through the Middle Fork Williams River valley to the mouth of Beechy Fork, where there is a small falls and swimming hole. Beechy Fork is a side stream of the Middle Fork Williams River and thus doesn't carry a lot of

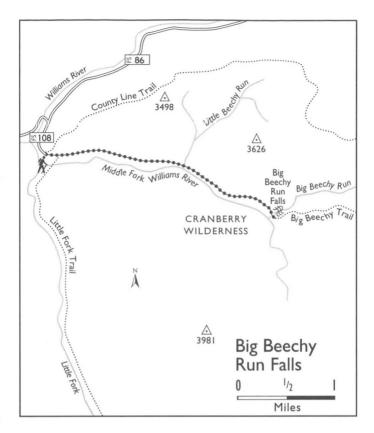

Big Beechy Run Falls

0   1/2   1
Miles

water, but the ten-foot-high falls are just one element of an overall attractive scene. Tall trees, rhododendron, rock outcrops, and two streams merging and creating light openings in the forest canopy make Beechy Run Falls an appealing setting.

Start your hike at the spot known as Three Forks—where the Williams River, Middle Fork, and Little Fork come together. Leave the parking area and immediately walk over a stream meander of the Middle Fork. Take a few steps into a clearing and come to the Little Fork Trail, which leaves to the right and follows an old roadbed and railroad grade. Leave the clearing, and pass a trailside kiosk on your left. Parallel a side stream on your left. A large wooded flat lies to your right alongside the Middle Fork. Enter a nearly grown-over clearing at 0.4 mile and continue beneath a woodland of tulip trees, sycamore, sugar maple, and hemlock. County Line Ridge rises sharply to your left.

Pass beside another clearing at 0.8 mile. Notice the rock bluff to your left. Step over two more stream meanders in succession. Cross a concrete culvert over a streambed at mile 1.4, then saddle up alongside the Middle Fork. The trail becomes pinched in by a bluff on your left and the Middle Fork on your right. Piled logs and debris in the river indicate the flooding potential of this usually clear mountain stream where trout are often visible in pools below.

The walking remains easy as you pass big boulders on the mountainside and in the stream, as the river winds close to and away from the trail. The former roadbed you are walking on often traces a railroad grade leftover from the logging days. Notice where the roadbed splits left and the grade stays forward along Middle Fork at mile 2.3. Come to Big Beechy Run at mile 2.4. Water from the stream flows over a flat slab of rock before dropping down into a clear pool, good for dipping. These falls will be at their finest during spring or after a big rain. In late summer and fall they will flow much slower. Just a few feet below the falls, Big Beechy Run merges with the Middle Fork to form a nice swimming hole.

Big Beechy Run Falls is the result of a "hanging" valley, created by differing rates of erosion. The primary stream of a valley—Middle Fork in this instance—cuts through the earth faster than tributaries like Big Beechy Run because it carries more water. Eventually, the erosion rate differential between the streams leaves the tributaries "hanging," resulting in a fall at the end of the tributary. Here, at the confluence of Middle Fork and Big Beechy Run, the water of Big Beechy Run has to drop precipitously to meet the Middle Fork.

Directions: From the Cranberry Visitor Center, 23 miles east of Richwood on WV 39/55, head north on WV 150, Highlands Scenic Highway, for 13.3 miles to Forest Service Road 86. Turn left on FS 86 and follow it for 11.5 miles to FS 108, just before the bridge over the Williams River. Turn left on FS 108 and follow it for 0.5

mile to dead end at the Three Forks Area. The Middle Fork Trail starts at the far end of the parking area.

Blue Knob

Scenery: ★★★   Difficulty: ★★★
Trail Condition: ★★★★   Solitude: ★★★
Children: ★★★
Distance: 5.8 miles round-trip
Hiking Time: 3:30 round-trip
Outstanding Features: attractive hardwood forest,
   some views

This hike takes you on the Pocahontas Trail, one of the area's least used pathways. Along this trail is an eye-appealing hardwood forest. From the Cranberry Visitor Center make a ridgeline climb to Blue Knob, where there are obscured views of the Cranberry country to the north from its 4,383-foot crest. The easy-to-follow treadway is well-graded and easy on the feet, but there is an overall elevation gain of 700 feet. Once you are away from the visitor center, the path is likely to be your own. The scenery is best in spring, when there are no leaves, or fall when the hardwoods show their colors. Leave the Cranberry Visitor Center parking area on the far side of the visitor center entrance, walk a path of stone steps a few feet, then follow a gravel treadway to a trail junction. Turn left and walk a few feet to a cleared overlook with some benches. Look down on the mountain valley of Stamping Creek. Return to the trail junction and continue forward, heading southwest on the Pocahontas Trail.

The trailside drops off sharply to the left of the level path. Intersect the Cranberry Nature Trail at 0.1 mile. Stay forward on the Pocahontas Trail, which soon swings past a precipice on trail left. There are more obscured views to the south. At 0.4 mile the path begins to ascend before intersecting the Buttrey Reserve Trail. Stay forward and continue to climb, slabbing up the north side of a ridge through a hardwood forest with little understory. This makes for

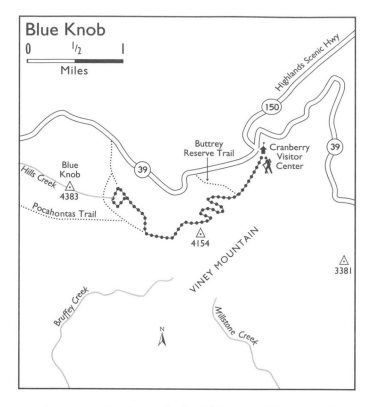

Blue Knob

0   1/2   1

Miles

Highlands Scenic Hwy

150

39

Buttrey Reserve Trail

Cranberry Visitor Center

Hills Creek

Blue Knob
4383

Pocahontas Trail

4154

VINEY MOUNTAIN

3381

Bruffey Creek

Millstone Creek

N

good scenery in the cathedral-like woodland. Make a series of switchbacks and achieve the top of the ridge at 1.3 miles.

The trail heads westerly for Blue Knob. Soon pass a spur trail leading to the Cranberry Mountain Lodge, located on private land. Stay forward and enjoy your progress atop a mountain flat. Pass a wildlife clearing on your right, then intersect the Blue Knob Trail at 2.2 miles. Turn right on the Blue Knob Trail, make a 0.2 mile climb, and level out on an arm of Blue Knob. Keep westerly up the north slope of the knob. At mile 2.7, the trail to the summit makes an acute left turn in a small clear area of the forest, while the Blue Knob Trail continues forward. Turn left on the trail to the summit and make your way up. Wind around Blue Knob to arrive at the top at mile 2.9. The summit is mostly wooded now, but there are some views to the north. You can see Highlands Scenic Highway on Black Mountain in the distance, and bits and pieces in other directions.

Directions: The trailhead starts at the Cranberry Visitor Center, 23 miles east of Richwood on West Virginia 39/55. Start your hike at the rear of the visitor center parking area.

Forks of Cranberry

Scenery: ★★★★★	Difficulty: ★
Trail Condition: ★★★	Solitude: ★★★
Children: ★★★	
Distance: 4.4 miles round-trip	
Hiking Time: 3:15 round-trip	
Outstanding Features: unusual forest, views	

The name Forks of Cranberry implies a watery hike. Actually this is a ridgetop walk to a rock outcrop with a view, and many other views along the way. The highland trail, located within the Cranberry Wilderness, is named Forks of Cranberry because it traces the ridge between the North and South Forks of the Cranberry River. The young forest, scattered

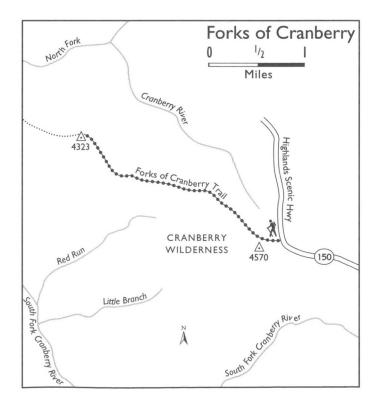

among the rocks on Black Mountain, is the end result of a natural disaster long ago.

Leave the parking area, enter the woods, and make a short climb past a trailside kiosk detailing the Cranberry Wilderness. Intersect an old road and walk up to a mountaintop field. The ridge of Kennison Mountain can be seen from the field. The path, however, skirts the right edge of the meadow, heads uphill, and enters a rocky section of trail. The forest—mountain-ash, red maple, mountain holly, and some red spruce—is low and seemingly stunted with an open canopy. Catawba rhododendron and mountain laurel crowd the trailside. The forest is still recovering from a devastating 1930s fire that burned the area to bare rock. After this fire, rains washed away what little soil was left, leaving little earth for trees to grow. Soil accumulation has been slow, by human standards, through erosion and wind, and moisture deposition. Of course, Mother Nature takes her sweet time.

At 0.7 mile enter a rock plain, where the forest is even thinner. Rock piles, known as cairns, mark the path through this open area dotted with small trees. Here, the trail gets fairly close to the right side of the ridge. Step that way and look north. The forest becomes more grown up past the rock plain, and the trail descends. A scree slope on your left at mile 1.2 offers more views, this time to the south. Watch for more views to your left in the next 0.2 mile. The forest becomes even larger and taller beyond the scree slope; beech becomes a major element of the now shady woodland.

Level out in a gap at 2.0 miles. Begin to climb up to an unnamed knob, swinging around its right flank. At mile 2.2, near the top of the 4,300-foot knob, the blue-blazed Forks of Cranberry Trail veers right. Another unmarked path leads forward a short distance to a rock outcrop on your left. Take the path to the outcrop. Up here, there are many views from the northeast to the southeast along the horizon, atop the sun-bleached white boulder jumble. Be careful as you make your way from rock to rock, as there are deep crevasses between these crags. Just as the forest is recovering all along this ridge, the spruce are growing here, and will eventually, on Mother Nature's timetable, crowd out this good view.

Directions: From the Cranberry Visitor Center, 23 miles east of Richwood on WV 39/55, head north on WV 150, Highlands Scenic Highway, for 5.2 miles to the Forks of Cranberry parking area, on your left.

High Rocks

Scenery: ★★★★★   Difficulty: ★
 Condition: ★★★★   Solitude: ★★★
Children: ★★★★
Distance: 3.6 miles round-trip
Hiking Time: 2:30 round-trip
Outstanding Features: great views, good picnic spot

This hike leads through an outstanding deciduous forest on a mostly level path to an inspiring overlook that makes an ideal picnic spot. Leave the Highlands Scenic Highway and meander on a wooded ridgetop with sizable trees. Your destination is a grassy flat beneath a shade-bearing red oak tree. This alluring flat happens to sit atop the edge of the High Rocks, which open south and east and offer views toward Old Virginia.

Enter the woods on a very level trail. The smooth gray trunks of beech trees and taller sugar maples crown the forest. Sugar maple leaves are easy to identify: they have U-shaped notches between their three lobes, as opposed to V-shaped notches between the lobes of red, mountain, and striped maples. Another big tree along the ridge is Northern red oak. Ferns cover the ground of the cathedral-like woodland. In other places, fallen trees have created light gaps, where the cycle of growth continues anew. The hiking is easy on the foot trail. Sawn logs serve as rest benches, or places to contemplate nature's beauty. Come to a grown-over woods road at mile 1.5. The trail turns right, follows the road a short distance, and turns left again. You may see a deer here.

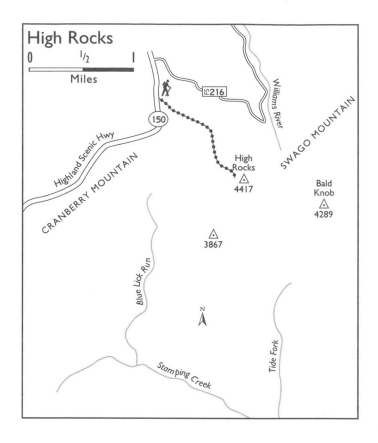

The trail switchbacks downhill, levels off, and continues southeast. At mile 1.7, pass two large oaks in succession just to the right of the path. Soon come to an attractive grassy clearing shaded by a red oak and ringed on the far side by a wood fence—this is the High Rocks. On the far side of the fence is an overhanging cliff. This is an ideal spot for a picnic, but keep younger hikers under close watch. The High Rocks stand at 4,240 feet.

The valley below is cut by the Greenbrier River. The villages down there are Mill Point, and Hillsboro, which is a little larger and farther to your right. Beyond the Greenbrier Valley are the Allegheny Mountains, which divide West Virginia from Old Virginia. The nearby mountain is Bald Knob.

Directions: From the Cranberry Visitor Center, 23 miles east of Richwood on WV 39/55, head north on

Falls of Hills Creek

Scenery: ★★★★★   Difficulty: ★★
Trail Condition: ★★★★★   Solitude: ★★
Children: ★★★★
Distance: 1.8 miles round-trip
Hiking Time: 1:15 round-trip
Outstanding Features: Three waterfalls, outstanding
  trail construction

This hike takes you down into the designated Falls of Hills Creek Scenic Area. Start on a paved, all-access path and cruise past big trees to the first of three falls. Beyond is an impressive and costly trail that uses wood and metal to allow access to two more falls along Hills Creek in a deep gorge. The third falls, Lower Falls, is West Virginia's second highest cataract.

Leave the parking area and begin descending on a paved, all-access trail into the 114-acre scenic area. Enter the woods and look for the many striped maples alongside the path. This understory tree has leaves resembling a goose foot and vertically striped bark. Striped maples rarely grow taller than 25 feet. In contrast, big beech and maple trees tower overhead. Pass the Fork Mountain Trail on your right and wind further into the woods, coming to the Upper Falls overlook at 0.3 mile. Upper Falls drops 25 feet off a ledge enveloped by hemlock trees. Beyond this overlook, the path turns to gravel. Continue on a gravel path, passing a shortcut back to the parking lot on your right and come to a wooden boardwalk, which drops into the rhododendron-lined valley by many steps.

Leave the boardwalk at 0.5 mile, and resume a gravel footpath, crossing an attractive arched footbridge over Hills Creek. Soon come to a viewing platform of wide Middle Falls on your right, which looks down on the watery drop. Leave this platform, then go down a metal stairwell astride a rock bluff. This metal contraption leads to another platform, offering

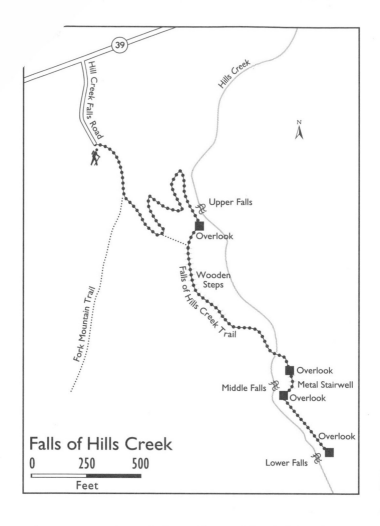

Falls of Hills Creek

0   250   500

Feet

a bottom-up view of the 45-foot falls dashing down onto a rock jumble.

Continue downstream on Hills Creek via another wooden boardwalk. The rock bluff continues to your left. Pass the upper end of Lower Falls on your right and descend on another set of wooden steps to view Lower Falls. This cataract is as narrow as Middle Falls is wide. It drops 63 feet and is West Virginia's second highest falls. Note the rockhouse to the right of the falls. The return trip requires a little more effort. Take the time to consider the elaborate trail construction, the likes of which I have never seen before.

Directions: From the Cranberry Visitor Center east of Richwood, drive 5.2 miles west on WV 39/55 to the Falls of Hills Creek Scenic Area, which will be on your left.

Meadow Creek Mountain

Scenery: ★★★★
Difficulty: ★★★
Trail Condition: ★★
Solitude: ★★★★★
Children: ★★
Distance: 4.8 miles round-trip
Hiking time: 3:00 round-trip
Outstanding Features: solitude, oak-hickory forest, view

This hike traces a little-used portion of the Allegheny Trail, a 330-mile path that runs the length of the Mountain State. This section of the Allegheny Trail climbs through an alluring woodland from Meadow Creek to the southwestern end of Meadow Creek Mountain, where there is a view. The trail is steep, which may account for its lack of use. Don't bypass this trek that is literally off the beaten path.

The trailhead is very elaborate for such a little-used section of trail. Leave the parking area and start northbound on the Allegheny Trail. You are actually traveling southwest, down an old woods road that parallels Lake Sherwood Road for a short distance before dipping in and out of a ravine onto Lake Sherwood Road. Cross the pavement, then walk over an arched footbridge that spans Meadow Creek. Follow the yellow blazes up two switchbacks, over-looking Meadow Creek at 0.3 mile.

Begin climbing through a forest that is much drier than most of the Monongahela National Forest. Meadow Creek Mountain is on the eastern edge of the national forest. The higher mountains to the west receive most of the eastbound frontal precipitation, resulting in a "rain shadow" for the mountains bordering Old Virginia. Thus, trees such as hickory, Virginia pine, chestnut oak, and sassafras are much more pre-

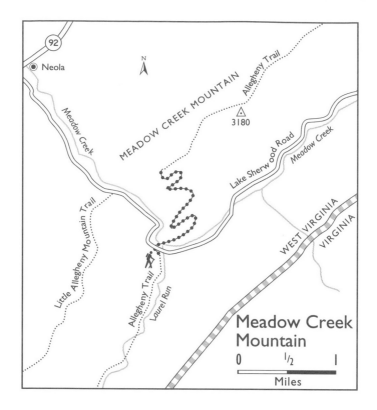

dominate here. Pass a rock bluff on your left at 0.4 mile. The ridgeline rises far to your left. Blown-down trees may be across the path, indicating lesser use and maintenance. The stateline ridge lies off to your right. Continue climbing, coming to the nose of a side ridge at 1.2 miles. There are obscured views to your right. Turn sharply left and keep climbing irregularly.

At mile 1.7, swing around the left side of a knob covered with Virginia pine, come to a gap, and switch over to the right side of the ridge. Keep climbing to a rock outcrop jutting from the mountainside on your left at mile 2.4. The Allegheny Trail makes an acute turn right. However, you walk just a few feet forward to a cleared overlook left. You have achieved the crest of Meadow Creek Mountain. Catch your breath then catch a view to the west. Down below is the valley of Meadow Creek. Across the way is Beaver Lick Mountain. Enjoy the solitude as you enjoy the scenery.

Directions: From exit 181 on I-64 at White Sulphur Springs, drive 15 miles north on State Road 92 to Neola. From Neola, travel east on Lake Sherwood Road for 2.5 miles and the parking area for the Allegheny Trail will be on your right.

Red Spruce Knob

Scenery: ★★★★   Difficulty: ★★
Trail Condition: ★★★★   Solitude: ★★★★
Children: ★★★★
Distance: 2.9 miles round-trip
Hiking Time: 2:00 round-trip
Outstanding Features: high country spruce woodland, view

For an interesting perspective of West Virginia's high elevation forest, take a walk to Red Spruce Knob, the highest point along the Highlands Scenic Highway, and only 160 feet shy of the Mountain State's highest point, Spruce Knob. There are no crowds here, and you have to work a little bit to get to the top. Up there, the knob's namesake grows in abundance amid mossy boulders. There is also a cleared view which looks off to the east from the mini-loop trail that encircles the pinnacle of Red Spruce Knob.

Leave the parking area, come to a trail sign, and veer left up the path marked with blue diamonds. Immediately climb around a ravine on your right, and begin a series of switchbacks among northern hardwoods, carpeted below in ferns. Ascend into an increasing number of red spruce until the trail levels out in a spruce flat at 0.4 mile. The trail winds along moderately, drifting over to the right side of the ridge in a mixed forest. At 1.0 mile, pass a gnarled sugar maple on your right, then make a brief jump up. Level off and resume climbing, arriving at Red Spruce Knob at 1.2 miles. Red spruce grow in abundance. But the understory is the story here. The story in a word is moss. Moss grows on everything—the ground, stumps, boulders, fallen trees—anything not moving fast.

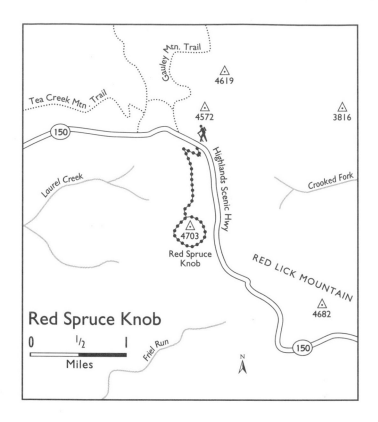

The trail now splits. Turn left and walk by a clearing on your right. Look in the clearing for the concrete foundations of a fire tower that once stood atop the knob. Drop down slowly among many fallen trees and come to an overlook on your left at mile 1.4. The cleared view offers views into the Crooked Fork valley.

Continue swinging around the knob. Notice the red spruce trees clinging atop the thin soils of the boulders here. These trees are subject to windthrow in this harsh environment and many will someday lie among their fallen brethren. Pass very close to the fire tower clearing and intersect the main trail again at mile 1.7. Stay left and head downhill 1.2 miles back to the trailhead.

Directions: From the Cranberry Visitor Center, 23 miles east of Richwood on WV 39/55, head north on WV 150, Highlands Scenic Highway, for 17.5 miles to the Red Spruce Knob parking area, on your right.

Part II:
Great Day Loops

▲▲▲

Dolly Sods–Otter Creek

Boars Nest Loop

Scenery: ★★★★★   Difficulty: ★★★
Trail Condition: ★★★   Solitude: ★★★
Children: ★
Distance: 7.3 miles round-trip
Hiking Time: 4:45 round-trip
Outstanding Features: views of Dolly Sods, highland
ecosystem

This hike loops through the Flatrock/Roaring Plains area, which is much like the heralded Dolly Sods, and actually adjoins the Dolly Sods, but receives lesser visitation. Climb up the South Fork Red Creek valley, then do a little walking on a gated forest road. Turn onto another trail, coming to the magnificent Flatrock Plains, where the spruce and heath forest is quite scenic. Before you leave the plains, grab a great view of the Dolly Sods to your north. Then drop steeply back down to South Fork Red Creek.

Start your climb by dropping down to South Fork Red Creek on the gated forest road by the parking area. This is the lower trailhead of South Prong Trail. Make an easy walk 0.5 mile down to the South Fork. Cross South Fork and turn left, tracing the watercourse upstream. Soon turn right, away from South Fork, climbing alongside a feeder rill to your right. Turn back up the main valley, picking up a logging grade at 0.9 mile. Follow the grade for 0.2 mile, then climb uphill to pick up a second logging grade at mile 1.4. This may seem confusing, but the trail is well-marked by blue plastic diamonds.

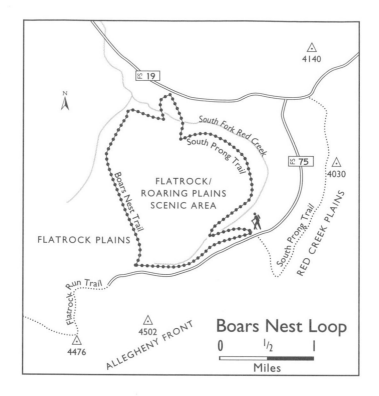

Boars Nest Loop

Stay with this grade as it ascends moderately up the South Fork valley. At mile 1.9, pass some rusty cables from timbering operations. Red spruce begin to make a presence at mile 2.3. Cross South Fork at mile 2.5, still climbing, now in a rhododendron thicket. At mile 2.9, leave the grade and clamber steeply to your right a short distance to closed Forest Service Road 70. This road is used to maintain a gas pipeline on leased national forest land. Turn right on FS 70. By mile 4.0, the roadside forest becomes predominately spruce.

At mile 4.3, pass a road leaving left. Just past this side road, on your right, is the Boars Nest Trail. Turn onto the Boars Nest Trail and enter the woods, coming to the headwaters of South Fork Red Creek at mile 4.4. Climb out of the watershed and onto the Flatrock Plains at mile 4.7. Low-lying shrubs such as mountain laurel and blueberry are punctuated with spruce, whose tops flag to the east, a reflection of the harsh and strong winds that fall upon this area, especially in winter.

Enjoy this beautiful stretch of trail on a pathway lined with stones, each lain one by one in front of one another. The canopy closes briefly at mile 4.9, and then the forest opens back up and fine views open up before you. The Dolly Sods lie dead-ahead to your north. There is an outcrop to your left at mile 5.2 that makes an ideal resting and viewing location.

Begin to drop off the Flatrock Plains, but not before getting a few more views, until you penetrate the tree canopy for good. Pass a spring branch and plunge downward through a yellow birch woodland. Make a pair of switchbacks at mile 5.8. Cross a logging grade at mile 6.4, and keep descending. A side stream of the South Fork is plainly audible and visible to your left. Come along the side stream, then cross the South Fork Red Creek at mile 7.0. Leave the creek bed, enter a clearing, and climb uphill through rocky woods. Intersect two old woods roads, before coming to the trailhead parking area, completing your loop at mile 7.3.

Directions: From Petersburg, drive south on WV 28 for 8.5 miles to Jordan Run Road (CR 28/7). Turn right on Jordan Run Road and follow it for 1 mile to Forest Service Road 19, which will be on your left. Turn left on FS 19 and follow it for 6.0 miles to FS 75. Turn left on FS 75 and follow it 2.5 miles to the Boars Nest/ South Prong trailhead. On the way, you will pass the upper South Prong trailhead. Start your hike at the lower South Prong trailhead.

Dunkenbarger Loop

Scenery: ★★★★	Difficulty: ★★★
Trail Condition: ★★★	Solitude: ★★★
Children: ★	
Distance: 7.6 miles round-trip	
Hiking Time: 4:45 round-trip	
Outstanding Features: high plateau environment, falls, wilderness setting	

This hike traverses the least-visited area of the Dolly Sods Wilderness. Start up Red Creek, then enter the valley of Little Stonecoal Run, where there is evidence

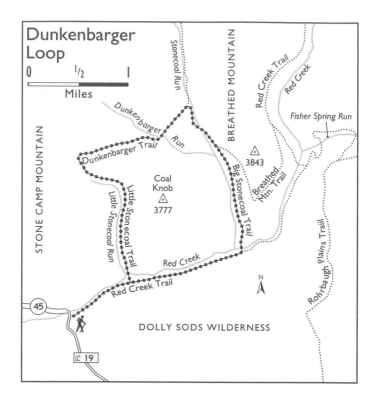

Dunkenbarger Loop

0   1/2   1
Miles

STONE CAMP MOUNTAIN

Dunkenbarger Trail

Dunkenbarger Run

Stonecoal Run

BREATHED MOUNTAIN

Red Creek Trail

Red Creek

Fisher Spring Run

△ 3843

Big Stonecoal Trail

Breathed Mtn. Trail

Coal Knob
△ 3777

Little Stonecoal Trail

Little Stonecoal Run

Red Creek

Red Creek Trail

Rohrbaugh Plains Trail

N

45

19

DOLLY SODS WILDERNESS

of logging days. Turn onto a high plateau via the Dunkenbarger Trail, which traverses a scenic menagerie of spruce woods, meadows, and heath glades. Intersect Big Stonecoal Run, and drop down this rugged valley back to Red Creek. You are likely to enjoy solitude everywhere, with the exception of Red Creek. There are two crossings of Red Creek, which can be overly high in spring and after major rains. However, Red Creek can usually be rock-hopped in summer and fall.

Leave the wooded parking area and head up the Red Creek Trail into the Dolly Sods Wilderness. Come right along Red Creek at 0.3 mile. The valley of Little Stonecoal Run is visible to your left. Leave the railroad grade you've been following and cross a feeder stream. Come to a meadow and trail junction at 0.6 mile. Turn left on the Little Stonecoal Trail. Cruise through a wooded flat and come to Red Creek. Ford Red Creek, angling your crossing slightly upstream, above Little Stonecoal Run coming in across the watercourse.

Pick up the footpath, marked by rock cairns, and begin climbing along the right bank of Little Stonecoal Run. You are now on a former logging road. Begin a steady ascent up the valley. At mile 1.1, look for a log skid road heading very steeply to your right. Keep forward and traverse a short rock jumble. Look for other skid roads heading up toward Coal Knob. Imagine the difficulty and danger associated with timbering such steep terrain! Pass a low rock bluff and small overhang on your right. At mile 1.7, turn away from the old road and make a rocky ascent. Come to a red pine stand just before intersecting the Dunkenbarger Trail at mile 2.4. The Little Stonecoal Trail just climbed 1,000 feet in 1.8 miles.

Turn right on the Dunkenbarger Trail, No. 558. Ascend moderately around a knob. Soon level out in evergreen woods. At mile 2.9, the forest canopy gives way to a heath glade of mountain laurel and blueberry bushes. Come to Dunkenbarger Run in a clearing at mile 3.4. This area is especially pretty, with grass, bushes, and trees all intermingled around the little stream. Follow the rock cairns across Dunkenbarger Run and keep heading east through a hodgepodge of spruce stands, heath glades, and small meadows. Step over a bog on a footlog at mile 3.8 and intersect the Big Stonecoal Trail at mile 4.0.

Turn right on the Big Stonecoal Trail and soon cross Big Stonecoal Run, heading downstream. Keep on a railroad grade as Big Stonecoal Run drops far off to your right. Intersect the Rocky Point Trail at mile 4.6, which comes at you on the railroad grade. However, drop sharply right down a footpath, still on the Big Stonecoal Trail, and immediately pass a side path to a rock outcrop with a view of a falls on Big Stonecoal Run. The stream is far below, but the noisy watercourse is clearly audible on the mountainside. Keep dropping and pick up another grade.

At mile 5.5, work around a slide that has eroded the railroad grade. Drop steeply down just before coming to Red Creek. At mile 5.9 the trail seemingly ends in a bluff. Make your way down to the water and make the stream crossing above the confluence of Big Stonecoal and Red creeks. Come to the Red Creek Trail at mile 6.0, just across the ford. Cut through some hemlock and rhododendron, then look for a path leaving the flat, and switchback up the rocky hillside in front of you. Ascend the hill, briefly pick up an old roadbed, and head downstream. Quickly leave the roadbed and follow a rocky, irregular path beneath maple and beech trees. Drop back down to the valley floor, and cross a small branch twice. Pick up a rail grade, passing a grassy clearing on your left at mile 6.5. Come to a second meadow and the Little Stonecoal Trail at mile 7.0. Retrace your steps down the Red Creek Trail back to the parking area, completing your loop at mile 7.6.

Directions: From Petersburg, drive south on West Virginia 28 for 8.5 miles to Jordan Run Road (CR 28/7). Turn right on Jordan Run Road and follow it for 1.0 miles to Forest Service Road 19, which will be on your left. Turn left on FS 19 and follow it for 6.0 miles to FS 75. Turn left on FS 75 and drive 3.7 miles to the hamlet of Laneville. Look on your right for a brown building with a sign that says, "Laneville Wildlife Cabin." Turn right here and immediately come to the Red Creek Trail.

Mylius Gap Loop

Scenery: ★★★★　　　Difficulty: ★★★
Trail Condition: ★★★　　Solitude: ★★
Children: ★
Distance: 9.4 miles round-trip
Hiking Time: 5:45 round-trip
Outstanding Features: pools and cascades,
　　some views, wilderness setting

This loop explores the high and the low of the Otter Creek Wilderness. Trace Otter Creek from its headwater as it cascades down the valley, gathering in pools down to where it gets big enough for swimming holes. Then climb out of the valley to Mylius Gap on Shavers

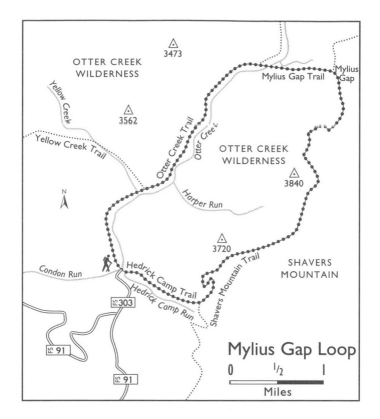

Mylius Gap Loop

0   1/2   1

Miles

Mountain. Make a solid climb to a high point on
Shavers Mountain, where there are some views along
the way. Drop back down to the Otter Creek valley via
the Hedrick Camp Trail. There will be other hikers
along Otter Creek, but after that you should enjoy
solitude.

Leave the Condon Run trailhead and follow the
gated road to a footbridge. Your return route, Hedrick
Camp Trail comes in through a rhododendron thicket to your right just before the footbridge. Cross
Condon Run, enter a field and continue on the road,
which leads down to a limestone treatment plant constructed to reduce acidity in Otter Creek and to improve the fish habitat. Stay on the road for 0.2 mile,
then turn left on the Otter Creek Trail, entering the
wilderness proper. Follow an old roadbed, flanked by
rhododendron.

Come alongside Otter Creek, then enter a clearing
at 1.0 mile. An old railroad bridge abutment is alongside Otter Creek. There are good views upstream here.

Turn left, tracing the grade, and step over sandy Yellow Creek. Enter a hemlock wood, then come to the Yellow Creek Trail at 1.2 miles. This junction is marked by a rock cairn, stones piled together.

Keep forward on the Otter Creek Trail, staying in hemlock woods. Rhododendron closes in on the path after a while. Many dry streambeds come in from your left, resulting in dips in the rail grade. At mile 2.0, open up to a clearing encircled by rhododendron. Next, climb up a bluff, passing beside a cabin-sized boulder. Drop back down to the grade briefly, then veer right at another clearing. Red Creek is just a few feet away at mile 2.2. Mountain laurel and rhododendron crowd the path as the canopy opens overhead. At mile 2.7, the railbed becomes very mucky. Take the trail up and to your left, bypassing this area.

Pass by a large clearing, drop back down to the rail grade, then intersect the Mylius Trail at mile 3.0. Turn right on the Mylius Trail, dropping down into a rhododendron thicket, and come to Otter Creek. Ford the stream and continue on the Mylius Trail. Step over several dry streambeds along the mild and shady upgrade. Climb east up to Mylius Gap on Shavers Mountain at mile 3.9. Turn right, following the Shavers Mountain Trail south.

The forest here is mixed, with drier species like oak interspersed with Fraser, magnolia, and hemlock. The climb is easy at first, and levels out, passing a property boundary marker at mile 4.6. Then begin switchbacking steeply up Shavers Mountain. The upgrade moderates in an evergreen thicket at mile 5.5, then ascends again through the shady woods. Top out at mile 5.9, after climbing 700 feet from Mylius Gap. Immediately lose elevation. There are obscured views to your left of the Glady Fork valley and Middle Mountain. Turn away from the ridge, skirting a knob to your left. Begin to see more property markers also to your left. Pick up an old roadbed at mile 6.8. The trail makes an easy downgrade. Leave the roadbed, and drop off the side of the ridge at mile 7.6. Make four switchbacks downhill. Pick up another roadbed coming in from your right, and intersect the Hedrick Camp Trail at mile 8.2.

Stay forward on the Hedrick Camp Trail. Shavers Mountain Trail veers up and away to your left. Come alongside the headwaters of Otter Creek. Leave the old roadbed at mile 9.0, dropping off to the left into rhododendron. Soon cross Otter Creek on a footbridge. Enter a hemlock wood and stay forward. Condon Run is on your right and a meadow is on your left. Emerge onto the closed forest road near the Condon Run trailhead. Turn left on the closed forest road, walk a few feet, and come to the Condon Run trailhead, completing your loop at mile 9.4.

Directions: From Elkins, drive east on US 33 for 11.5 miles to Stuart Memorial Drive, Forest Service Road 91, at Alpena Gap on Shavers Mountain. Turn left on FS 91 and follow it for 1.1 miles to a junction. Stay forward at the junction, now on FS 303, and dead-end at the Condon Run trailhead in 0.4 mile.

Spruce Knob-Laurel Fork Area

Camp Five Run Loop

Scenery: ★★★★★	Difficulty: ★★★
Trail Condition: ★★★	Solitude: ★★★★★
Children: ★★★	
Distance: 6.3 miles round-trip	
Hiking Time: 4:00 round-trip	
Outstanding Features: huge meadow, great views	

This loop is a feast for the eyes nearly every step of the way as it passes through the Laurel Fork South Wilderness. Leave the ridge of Middle Mountain and drop down along Camp Five Run. There are numerous meadows along the way. Turn up Laurel Fork, then enter a huge meadow with great views of the valley and surrounding mountains. Climb back up to the

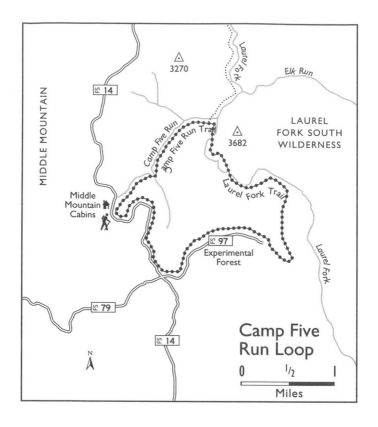

Camp Five
Run Loop

0   1/2   1

Miles

high country to an experimental forest area where there are more views. End your loop with a walk along a quiet forest road.

Be advised: portions of the trails along this loop can be hard to follow, but with a little reckoning you should have no problem. Leave Forest Service Road 14 and walk down the gravel road a short distance to the Middle Mountain Cabins on your right. Keep on the former railroad bed as it passes a dammed pond, and enter the Laurel Fork South Wilderness at 0.2 mile. Keep following the grade downhill through a spruce wood, then cross over Camp Five Run at 0.6 mile.

Step across Camp Five Run twice in succession at 0.7 mile, then enter a field. Make a fourth crossing at 0.9 mile. You are now on the right bank of Camp Five Run. The trail soon climbs away from the grade and follows a foot trail, only to regain the railroad grade. Leave the railroad grade a second time for good at mile 1.2, where the trail splits off to the right. There is a large meadow to your left.

The footpath stays in the woods as the meadow to your left increases in size. At mile 1.5, come to a wooden post indicating the intersection with the Laurel Fork Trail, No. 306. This is the end of the Camp Five Run Trail. The meadow below you, across Camp Five Run, makes a nice, relaxing spot. To continue the loop, veer right on the Laurel River Trail, drop down through a red pine and spruce woodland and pick up a rail bed. Here are field, fern, and forest, with much evidence of beavers: still ponds and chewed-down trees.

Cross Laurel Fork in an open field at 1.7 miles. Reenter the woods, then watch for the trail splitting left, still heading upstream along another road bed. Follow this grassy path, ignoring other trails dropping down to Laurel Fork at 2.0 miles. One of these errant trails has a capped well on it. Stay forward on the roadbed to cross a little flowing rill coming in from your left at 2.1 miles. Just ahead is another streambed, most likely dry, that comes in from your left through a clearing. On the far side of the streambed is a red pine plantation. Walk forward to this dry streambed and follow it down toward Laurel Fork. There, another roadbed heads left—upstream. Follow this grassy roadbed into the pine plantation. The wide road winds beneath the needle-carpeted woods, and then enters a big meadow, coming directly to Laurel Fork at 2.5 miles. Cross Laurel Fork and turn left, following the roadbed upstream along the right side of the meadow. There are great views of the valley and surrounding ridges to the south in this open area. The trail, passing through mostly open terrain, becomes somewhat wooded again as it crosses an unnamed tributary coming in from your right at mile 2.9. Just after this crossing the trail turns up and to your right away from the meadow to parallel the tributary you just crossed, and steepens as it leaves the meadow. The forest canopy closes overhead and spruce trees increase in number.

At mile 3.4, the trail swings right around the head of a hollow and continues to climb. Come to trail signs and gated Forest Service Road 97 at mile 3.8. Turn right on the forest road. Along this road, closed to the public, is an ongoing tree farming experiment. Views to the south and southwest open up at miles 3.9 and 4.2. Meander along the ridge and pass a gate and signs explaining the tree experiments, coming to FS 14 at mile 4.9. You are now 3,700 feet high. Turn right on FS 14 and head north, passing the Lynn Knob Trail on your left at mile 6.0. Then, come to the gravel road of the Middle Mountain Cabins, completing your loop at 6.3 miles.

Directions: From Elkins, drive east on US 33 for 12.6 miles over Alpena Gap to the hamlet of Alpena. Turn right on Glady Road, County Road 27 (just across from the Alpine Motel). Follow Glady Road for 9.2 miles to Glady. Turn left on Middle Mountain Road (Forest Service Road 422) and drive for 4.6 miles to FS 14. Turn right on FS 14 and follow it south for 4.5 miles to the Middle Mountain Cabins, which are on your left. The Camp Five Run Trail starts on the gravel road leading down to the cabins.

Horton/Spring Ridge Loop

Scenery: ★★★★   Difficulty: ★★★
Trail Condition: ★★★★   Solitude: ★★★★
Children: ★★
Distance: 6.7 miles round-trip
Hiking Time: 4:15 round-trip
Outstanding Features: historic travel route, wildlife
   clearings, some views

This is a classic stream and ridge loop hike. Start by ascending up the very pretty Lower Two Spring Run valley along an old wagon road that used to connect the hamlets of Horton, on Gandy Creek, and Riverton, on South Branch Potomac River. Briefly take the Allegheny Mountain Trail to the Spring Ridge Trail, where there are wildlife clearings a-plenty. Your return trip to Gandy Creek is a pleasant woodland stroll. Though the grades aren't terribly steep, there

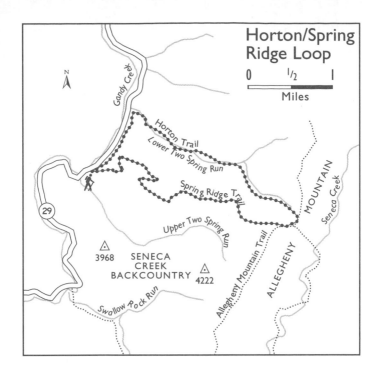

Horton/Spring Ridge Loop

are few level sections along this circuit.

Leave the parking area on the Horton Trail and pass through a clearing, coming to Lower Two Spring Run. Enter the woods and veer right, walking uphill on a roadbed. Follow the blue diamonds along the right bank of the stream. At 0.2 mile, briefly leave the road, circumventing a washed-out area. Keep up the rocky valley, which lies beneath a hardwood forest with a light understory. Bypass another washout at 0.4 mile. Watch for some sizable oaks in the lower section of this valley. Cross Lower Two Spring Run at 0.6 mile and 0.9 mile, once again picking up the roadbed. Stay directly alongside the stream, which drops steeply, resulting in numerous cascades that are pleasing to the eye. Cross the stream twice more at mile 1.1. You are now on the right bank, where a faint path comes in on your right. Stay forward, veering uphill just below a fork in the stream. The Horton Trail now climbs along the right fork. Come alongside the right fork rill, as the path rises sharply. Step back and forth over the streamlet, then come to a trail junction at mile 2.7. Stay right, now on the Allegheny Trail, and walk just a few feet to another trail junction. The Horton Trail leaves left down to Seneca Creek. Stay right, still on the Allegheny Trail, and keep climbing, skirting a sloped wildlife clearing. Reenter the woods just before coming to a third trail junction at mile 3.0. Turn acutely right, now on the Spring Ridge Trail.

This wide, grassy lane makes for easy walking. Drop moderately to a clearing at mile 3.4. The trail then levels off and passes another clearing. Watch for a side trail to a wildlife watering pond at mile 3.8. Soon come to another wildlife clearing at mile 4.0. Slip over to the right-hand side of the ridge and keep descending. There are some views off to your right of the Gandy Creek valley and Middle Mountain. Traverse a hemlock grove. At mile 4.6, pass a very small clearing and pond. Make a switchback to the right, then to the left, and begin to parallel a small stream on trail right. The path drops sharply then levels off, as the stream continues to descend.

At mile 5.4, pass a castle-like rock outcrop to your left. Gandy Creek becomes audible below. After leaving the Spring Ridge Trail, come to County Road 29 at mile 5.9. Turn right on the gravel road and mostly descend, coming to the Horton Trail parking area at mile 6.7, completing your loop.

Directions: From the town of Seneca Rocks, head south on US 33 for 13 miles to Briery Gap Road. Turn right on Briery Gap Road and follow it up for 2.5 miles to Forest Service Road 112. Turn right on FS 112 and head up 13.2 miles to FS 1. Turn right on FS 1 and follow it 4.1 miles to County Road 29. Stay right and follow CR 29 for 9.3 miles to a parking area on your right. A nearby sign says "Potomac Cooperative Wildlife Management Area." The Horton Trail starts just beyond the spruce trees by a clearing.

North Prong Loop

Scenery: ★★★★   Difficulty: ★★★
Trail Condition: ★★★   Solitude: ★★★★
Children: ★★
Distance: 6.4 miles round-trip
Hiking Time: 3:45 round-trip
Outstanding Features: meadows, stream walking,
   beaver dams, a few views

This trail loops through the south side of the Seneca Creek Backcountry, which is within the Spruce Knob-Seneca Rocks National Recreation Area. Start on the wide Allegheny Mountain Trail for some easy walking to the North Prong Trail. Drop down to North Prong of Big Run, passing a scenic mountain meadow. Keep descending in the intimate valley of North Prong to Big Run. Return to Allegheny Mountain along Big Run, where there is an elongated meadow that offers ridgeline vistas. There are numerous crossings of North Prong that can be rock-hopped in times

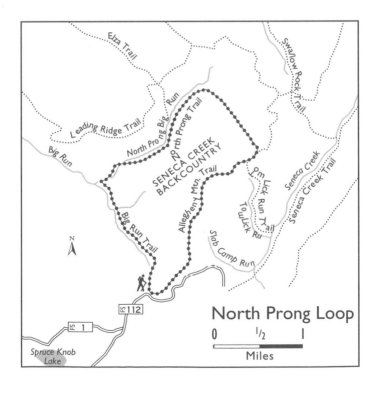

of normal stream flow. There is also one steep section at the end of the hike.

Start your loop on the Allegheny Mountain Trail. This is a gated forest road infrequently used by forest service personnel to maintain wildlife food plots located in the backcountry. Other small roads splinter off the main path, which is easy to follow, being marked with blue diamonds. Overhead is a northern hardwood forest of maple, birch, and beech. Undulate along the ridgeline at around 4,000 feet. At 0.7 mile, a side trail leads right from a gap to a wildlife clearing. Keep forward and climb, passing a side road marked "532 S" at 1.4 miles. Intersect the Tom Lick Run Trail at mile 2.0, which leaves to your right. Continue forward on the Allegheny Mountain Trail.

At mile 2.2, come to the North Prong Trail. There is a grassy clearing here and some pine trees. Veer left on the North Prong Trail, leaving the clearing behind. Ascend to a another clearing, then begin a steady descent, coming to a large meadow at mile 3.0, which meadow slowly narrows to the valley of North Prong. There are beaver dams on the stream.

Come to a junction at mile 3.7. The Leading Ridge Trail crosses North Prong on a bridge. Stay forward, still on the North Prong Trail. Soon cross North Prong twice and stay creekside in the boulder-strewn valley. Skirt a clearing and red pine plantation at a feeder stream. Cross this feeder stream and cross North Prong three more times, coming to another clearing and the Big Run Trail at mile 4.9. Turn left on the Big Run Trail, which meanders through a meadow dotted with trees. The valley briefly becomes fully forested, then breaks up into an irregular clearing that runs up the valley. This open area is long and wide enough to avail ridgeline views of the surrounding mountainsides. Look for occasional beaver dams. The path stays on the north edge of the meadow, sometimes under canopy, sometimes not.

At mile 5.7, slosh across a trio of tiny tributaries coming in from the left, and then step over a larger stream at mile 5.8. Just past this is a spruce plantation.

Begin a climb that gradually steepens and ends at the Allegheny Mountain trailhead, completing your loop at mile 6.4.

Directions: From the town of Seneca Rocks, head south on US 33 for 13 miles to Briery Gap Road. Turn right on Briery Gap Road and follow it up for 2.5 miles to Forest Service Road 112. Turn right on FS 112 and head up 12.8 miles to the Allegheny Mountain trailhead, which is on your right. The Allegheny Mountain Trail starts at the back of the parking area.

Cranberry Area

Black Mountain Loop

Scenery: ★★★★	Difficulty: ★★
Trail Condition: ★★★	Solitude: ★★★★
Children: ★★	

Distance: 4.6 miles round-trip
Hiking Time: 3:30 round-trip
Outstanding Features: fern fields, good views, logging camp relics

This is a lesser-used high country hike on a relatively new trail. It leaves Williams River Overlook then drops off the east side of Black Mountain to intersect an old logging grade, which passes through incredible, continuous fern fields. Emerge onto an interpretive boardwalk at Big Spruce Overlook, then cross Highland Scenic Highway to enter the Cranberry Wilderness. Loop back around on less sloping terrain to Williams River Overlook, crossing the highway one more time. Though you are near a road, few people venture from their cars to walk Black Mountain. Make this circuit in the summer to enjoy the vast fern fields.

The trail starts near the restrooms at Williams River Overlook at 4,400 feet. To the north you can see the Big Spruce Overlook, the halfway point of this loop. Climb a bank and actually head south, away from Big Spruce, through a mixed woodland,

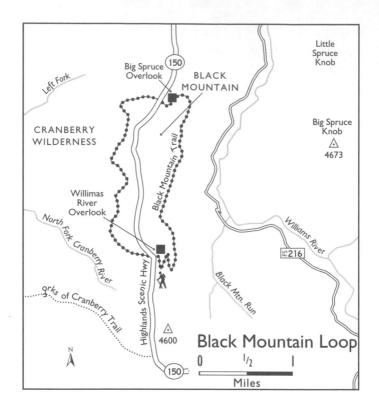

broken with rocks. Listen for the chatter of northern red squirrels as they scold you for entering their domain. Pass between mossy boulders and begin to descend the steep, east slope of Black Mountain via switchbacks. This narrow footpath turns north near the 4,000 foot elevation. At 0.6 mile come to your first fern field, which covers the forest floor. Overhead are yellow birch, beech, and black cherry. Make your way up and down to intersect an old logging grade at 1.1 miles. The footing is easier, with fewer vertical variations. Trees cover much of the grade, but the trail is easily passable. Soon come to a split in the grade. Take the upper grade to your left and continue north.

Cross a series of seeps on footlogs at mile 1.4. Begin to look for rusty tubs and other implements indicating a former logging camp. The main area of the camp is in an immense fern meadow just past the seep. Next, come to a view to your right of Williams River watershed and Big Spruce Knob at mile 1.6.

While walking along the grade, look for lumps of coal and rotted crossties. Leave the old grade at mile 2.1 and turn left, climbing to a wooden boardwalk that is part of Big Spruce Overlook. Turn right on the boardwalk for a good view, and then backtrack on the boardwalk, coming out at the Big Spruce Overlook at mile 2.3. Look south toward Williams River Overlook. Stay on the right-hand side of the parking area and cross the highway at the Black Mountain Trail sign.

Begin heading southward on a footpath through low trees and open areas. Enter a spruce wood at mile 2.6, dropping briefly and sharply at mile 2.9. Beyond this, the mostly level terrain makes up for the root and rock-laden trail. More fern fields lie beneath hardwood areas. Come to a rock jumble at mile 3.3, then dance between truck-sized boulders, beginning a steady downward grade for 0.4 mile. Swing around a knob to your left, then climb a hill interspersed with rocks and trees. Look back for views into the Cranberry Wilderness. Below you is the North Fork Cranberry River. Emerge onto the Highland Scenic Highway and the Williams River Overlook at mile 4.6, completing your loop.

Directions: From the Cranberry Visitor Center, 23 miles east of Richwood on WV 39/55, head north on WV 150, Highlands Scenic Highway, for 6.3 miles to the Williams River Overlook, on your right. The Black Mountain Trail starts near the overlook restrooms.

Cowpasture Loop

Scenery: ★★★★★	Difficulty: ★★
Trail Condition: ★★★★	Solitude: ★★★
Children: ★★★	

Distance: 7.4 miles round-trip
Hiking time: 3:45 round-trip
Outstanding Features: open glades, former prison camp, beaver dams, good birding

This loop circles the Cranberry Glades Botanical Area. It offers glimpses into a glades ecosystem that is the most southerly tundra environment in the country. There are also views of the surrounding mountains as you trace a nearly level course well above 3,000 feet. One open area still has traces of a former World War II prison camp. A side hike on the Cranberry Glades Boardwalk will enhance this already interesting loop, which is included in the trail mileage.

Start your hike on an old road leading easterly. Pass a clear area on your left, then enter a northern hardwood forest of black cherry, yellow birch, and maple. The trail is lined with rhododendron. Cross a small branch just before intersecting the Thomas Reserve Trail at 0.4 mile. Keep forward on the level trail and come to a large clearing, with built-up bird boxes. Cross a stream on a wooden bridge and come to old Forest Service Road 980 at 0.9 mile. Old FS 980 leads southeast to the Cranberry Visitor Center.

Notice the crumbling blacktop and concrete laid into the clearing. This area was the site of an old World War II prison camp where Germans were held. Now, turn left, staying on the Cowpasture Trail, and cross Charlies Creek on a wood bridge, turning left yet

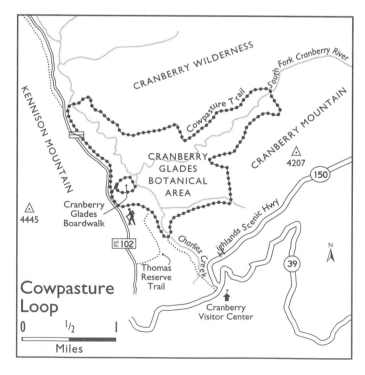

again. The Cowpasture Trail has circled back, now following Charlies Creek downstream briefly before resuming an easterly tack.

The hiking remains easy through a rhododendron tunnel and shady woods. Cross small streams on footbridges at miles 1.9 and 2.1. Lope over a small ridge, then come to a clearing with views of Kennison Mountain above. Watch for a sharp left turn in the clearing at mile 2.8. The path leaves the old roadbed and descends to South Fork Cranberry River at mile 2.9. Notice the beaver dams on the stream.

Climb away from the South Fork Cranberry to rejoin another roadbed, now heading westerly. The trail undulates more here, passing through glades, hardwoods, and evergreens. Look for the many hawthorn trees, which are a short, bushy softwood with one-inch thorns on their branches. The hawthorn thrives in these mixed areas, especially near clearings. Cross a wooden bridge at mile 3.9, continuing moderate ups and downs. Another wooden bridge is crossed at mile 4.8. Look for more beaver ponds to your left, while crossing three more wooden bridges in succession.

At mile 5.1, a side trail leads left to an elevated viewing deck where you can see more beaver ponds. This is also a good birding locale. Return to the main trail and cross more wooden bridges, including one over South Fork Cranberry River at mile 5.5. Reenter the woods to emerge on gated Forest Service Road 102. Turn left on FS 102 and follow it 0.2 mile to a gate. Continue up FS 102 and come to the Cranberry Glades Interpretive Boardwalk, on your left at mile 6.7. Take this 0.5-mile side trail and learn about the unique nature of the Cranberry Glades via the informative displays. Return to FS 102, turn left, and walk 0.2 mile, completing your loop.

Directions: From the Cranberry Visitor Center, 23 miles east of Richwood on WV 39/55, head west on WV 39/55 for 0.25 mile to Forest Service Road 102. Turn right on FS 102 and follow it for 1.3 miles to the south terminus of the Cowpasture Trail, which will be on your right.

Gauley Mountain Loop

Scenery: ★★★★	Difficulty: ★★
Trail Condition: ★★★★	Solitude: ★★★★
Children: ★★★	

Distance: 7.7 miles round-trip
Hiking Time: 4:15 round-trip
Outstanding Features: easy hiking, well marked trail,
    meadows, some views

This hike heads through the highlands of the Tea Creek Backcountry. Start at 4,200 feet on the Gauley Mountain Trail and do some ridge walking. Then drop down the attractive valley of Red Run to Right Fork Tea Creek. Cruise along Right Fork past beaver dams and meadows to compete the loop. There are no steep sections and the trails are well-marked and maintained. These conditions are ideal for novice hikers. Experienced trekkers can also enjoy this high country circuit that only briefly dips below 4,000 feet.

Start your hike on the Gauley Mountain Trail, entering the forest on an old woods road. Immediately come to a clearing and pass over three small rills on wood bridges. Wind through a young forest of spruce, beech, and cherry. Pass a clearing, reenter the woods, and dip down to cross a stream on a wooden bridge. Come to the Right Fork Connector Trail just past this stream, at 0.4 mile. This is your return route. The handy metal maps at every trail junction make getting lost a chore. Keep forward on the Gauley Mountain Trail. This old grade leads moderately up the west slope of Gauley Mountain. Cross a wooden bridge and pass through clearings at miles 1.4 and 2.1. Soon begin a downgrade, coming to the Red Run Trail at mile 2.6. Turn left on the Red Run Trail, heading west on a very rooty path beneath a spruce forest. Pass a small clearing and come alongside the upper reaches of Red Run at mile 3.3. You are now on an old railgrade, which crosses a feeder branch of Red Run at

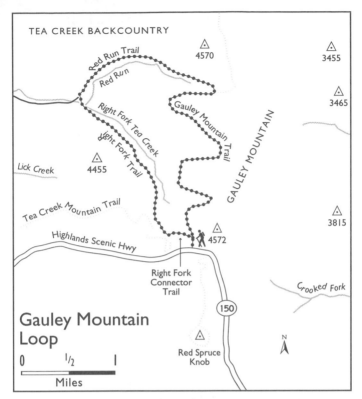

TEA CREEK BACKCOUNTRY

Red Run Trail

Red Run

4570

3455

3465

Right Fork Tea Creek

Gauley Mountain Trail

Light Fork Trail

GAULEY MOUNTAIN

Lick Creek

4455

Tea Creek Mountain Trail

3815

Highlands Scenic Hwy

4572

Right Fork
Connector
Trail

Crooked Fork

150

Gauley Mountain Loop

0   ¹/₂   1

Miles

Red Spruce Knob

N

mile 3.6. Note the remains of a bridge here. The trail briefly detours around a mucky stretch of the grade. Pick your way through a very rocky section of trail as Red Run drops far below in the valley off to your left. At mile 4.5, swing to your right and cross a feeder stream. Shortly cross a second stream on a log footbridge. The old grade keeps a straight path, then makes a sharp switchback at mile 5.0. Descend just a bit more, coming to the Right Fork Trail at mile 5.1.

Stay forward, now on the Right Fork Trail. Step over Red Run, then climb alongside Right Fork. At mile 5.5, cross the now much smaller stream. Enter a clearing surrounded by spruce. Meadows and beaver dams become a feature on Right Fork. Come to a trail junction at mile 6.7. For a good view turn right, staying on the Right Fork Trail, and take a short side trip to Tea Creek Meadow. This clearing offers views of Gauley Mountain. Return to the junction and take the Right Fork Connector Trail to intersect the Gauley Mountain Trail at mile 7.3. Turn right on the Gauley

Mountain Trail, retracing your steps, and come to the Gauley Mountain trailhead at mile 7.7, completing your loop.

Directions: From Marlinton, drive north on US 219 for 7.0 miles to Highlands Scenic Highway. Turn left on Highland Scenic Highway and follow it south for 6.2 miles to the Gauley Mountain trailhead, on your right. If you come to the Little Laurel Overlook, backtrack 0.5 mile to the trailhead.

Stateline Loop

Scenery: ★★★★	Difficulty: ★★★
Trail Condition: ★★★★	Solitude: ★★
Children: ★★	
Distance: 10.2 miles round-trip	
Hiking Time: 6:30 round-trip	
Outstanding Features: lake and mountain views	

This loop hike traverses three distinct environments. Start your trek on the shores of Lake Sherwood, West Virginia's prettiest lake. Then make a streamside walk along Meadow Creek. Climb up to the high ridge that forms the boundary between West Virginia and Virginia. Travel south along the state line and enjoy views into both states. Then drop back down to the Lake Sherwood to complete your loop.

There are very few steep sections on the state line ridge, and the ascent from Lake Sherwood to the state line is very gradual. The main challenge is the mileage. Take your time and make a day of it. Be aware that there is no more available water after you leave Meadow Creek. You are nearly certain to have company along Lake Sherwood, but after that the loop will probably be yours.

Leave the parking area near the picnic area restrooms and cross a little wooden footbridge. Turn left at the Lake Sherwood sign. Follow the path to another trail junction. Turn right, as the footpath left leads back to the hiker parking area. Walk just a few more

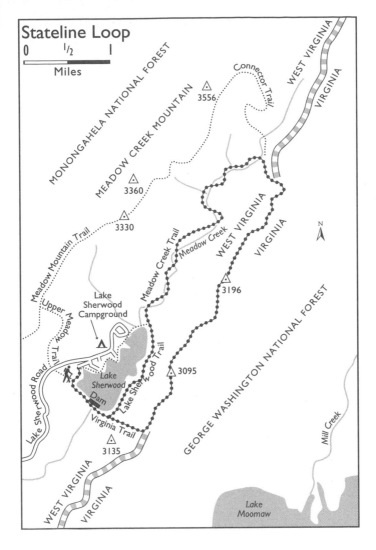

feet and come to Lake Sherwood Trail. Turn right again and begin tracing the shore of Lake Sherwood, which is on your left. Swing around a cove and intersect a forest road at 0.4 mile. Keep forward and cross the dam holding back the lake. There are great views back to the northeast of the mountain impoundment and Meadow Creek Mountain on your left.

Cross over the Spillway Bridge, make a brief climb, and come to a trail junction at 0.7 mile. To your right is the Virginia Trail, your return route. Stay left on the Lake Sherwood Trail. The white pine woodland offers many views into the lake as it undulates over small ridges and mostly dry stream beds. Many relaxation and repose benches sit alongside the trail. Come to the Meadow Creek Trail at mile 2.1, just before the foot-bridge over Meadow Creek. Turn right here and begin a moderate ascent alongside the pretty stream. More pine woods continue, with an understory of rhodo-dendron and mountain laurel. Make the first of many creek crossings in 0.3 mile. These can all be easily rock-hopped in times of normal flow. Make four more fords in the next mile.

The crossings continue as Meadow Creek becomes ever smaller. Vegetation crowds the path, making the walk seem at times like a jungle trek. Emerge onto an old woods road at mile 4.8 onto the Connector Trail. Turn right on the Connector Trail and leave the rhodo-dendron behind. A hickory-oak forest grows here above an understory rife with mountain laurel. In 0.1 mile the old road splits; stay forward. Soon come to a game clear-ing. Head directly across the grassy field, then look for the blue blazes at the clearing's end, slightly to your left. Come to the Allegheny Mountain Trail and the state line at mile 5.1. Turn right on the Allegheny Mountain Trail, heading upward and southerly along an old fire road. Begin to roll up and over small knobs and down to gaps among the hickories and oaks. Note the many blueberry bushes along the trail, which will be fruiting in late July. Also look overhead at the many large acorn-bearing oaks, that along with the blueber-ries, provide much food for wildlife.

At mile 6.1, an old road heads straight, while the Allegheny Mountain Trail dives off the ridge to your right. This is the only very steep section of the loop and it ends quickly. Swing around the right side of a rock house. Just past this rock house, you can climb this very outcrop to your left and garner some very good views of Virginia's Blue Ridge. Resume south-ward, riding the knife-edged rock uplift. The tread-way is tough but the views into both states demand a slow pace. Eventually, the ridge widens out and the trail becomes more foot-friendly. At mile 7.4, in a gap, look for Lake Moomow to your left. This is a recreation area in Virginia's George Washington National Forest, much like Lake Sherwood.

Ahead are still more views of Lake Moomow. At mile 8.0, the trail widens as it again traces an old fire road. Another old road comes in from your left at mile 8.3; stay forward and begin the most continuous climb of the hike. Top out on a knob, and descend to the Virginia Trail at mile 8.9. Turn right on the Virginia Trail and drop steeply. The descent moderates when it picks up an old road and parallels a streambed to your right. Turn away from the stream before intersecting the Lake Sherwood Trail at mile 9.5. Continue forward, now on the Lake Sherwood Trail, and retrace your steps over the spillway bridge, crossing the dam, and coming to the picnic area trailhead, completing your loop at mile 10.2.

Directions: From exit 181 on I-64 at White Sulphur Springs, drive 15.0 miles north on State Road 92 to Neola. From Neola, travel east on Lake Sherwood Road for 11.0 miles and come to the recreation area. Turn right just before coming to the campground entrance booth and head toward the picnic area. Follow this paved road a short distance to another right to the hiker parking area. The Lake Sherwood Trail leaves near the picnic area restrooms.

Part III:
Great
Overnight Loops

▲▲▲

Dolly Sods–Otter Creek

Canaan Backcountry Overnight Loop

Scenery: ★★★★   Difficulty: ★★
Trail Condition: ★★★   Solitude: ★★★
Children: ★★
Distance: 2.4, 9.1, 6.7 miles each day
Hiking Time: 1:30, 4:45, 3:30 hours each day
Outstanding Features: some views, high country
    spruce woods, trail shelters

This loop takes place atop the high elevation plateau of Canaan Mountain, in the 13,532-acre Canaan Mountain Backcountry. The elevations here range from 3,100 feet to 4,145 feet. This high country more closely resembles Canada than West Virginia in its plant life. The trails here are gentle on this plateau, making this a good opening backpack trip to start the season, or when a veteran wants to break-in a novice. Leave your tent behind on this hike. Trail shelters, where you'll be staying each night, make trips in iffy weather more promising. The first day is short, which is good if you lack time or want an easy beginning.

Start your loop on Fire Trail No. 3 (Forest Trail No. 104). Head south at a slight decline through a thicket of mountain laurel and rhododendron. Blue diamonds mark the trail, as they do on all the trails in the Canaan Backcountry. At 0.3 mile cross a small creek on a tiny stone footbridge and keep descending. The overstory now is tall spruce. Make a short, steep descent just before coming to the Plantation Trail at 0.8 mile. Turn left on the Plantation Trail (FT No. 101), named after the Civilian Conservation Corps planted red spruce here. The original forest was logged from 1890–1910. Terrible fires followed the logging before it became part of the Monongahela National Forest. When it did, the CCC also cut in the fire roads, like the one you just hiked on, that are now numbered in sequence.

There are more hardwoods here, maple, yellow birch, and black cherry. These are components of the

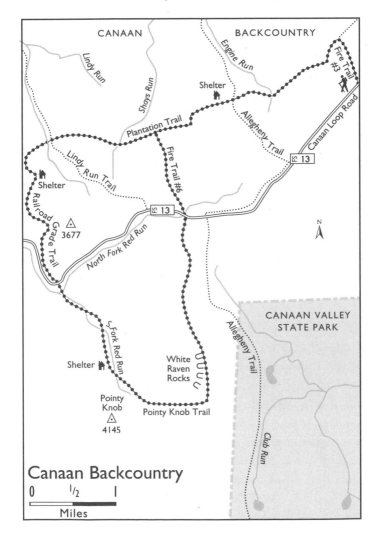

northern hardwood forest. Cross a small stream at 0.9 mile and soon begin a brief, moderate climb. Cross a gas-line cut at mile 1.3 and reenter the woods, passing an outcrop at mile 1.7. Climb the rocks and get views to your north, and then drop down to Engine Run. Next, swing around a knob to your left, traversing a rocky footbed with an open understory before coming to the Allegheny Trail at mile 2.4. The Allegheny Trail is a long-distance path running from Virginia to Pennsylvania. Pass just a short distance through this junction and see the side trail leading right to the trail shelter that is your first night's destination. This three-sided wood shelter with an open front faces a small spring branch that is your water source.

Start day two by keeping west on the Plantation Trail and immediately cross the spring branch which provides water for the shelter, then pass through a boggy glade. Walk on a raised footbed of gravel and logs. The spruce gives way to another evergreen—hemlock—which is characterized by flat needles with a white stripe underneath, and vertically fissured bark. Cross two small streams at miles 3.0 and 3.4 of your loop hike. Notice the small concrete dam on the second creek. These dams were also installed by the CCC to water the planted trees and to fight fires.

At mile 3.6, come to Fire Trail No. 6 (Forest Trail No. 108). Turn left here and begin a gentle ascent, entering a dark spruce woodland carpeted with needles and moss. Pass another fire road going to seed at mile 4.2. The forest opens overhead as you descend to Canaan Loop Road at mile 4.6. Turn left, crossing North Fork Red Run. Notice the row of red pines lining the road-way. These were also planted by the CCC and are not area natives. About 50 yards up the road, turn right on another gravel road, which leaves the clearing and comes to the Pointy Knob Trail (FT No. 139). This trail leaves the roadbed and turns left up a hill. The mild ascent is off and on. The rocky treadway slows you down, as do occasional mucky spots.

Come to the White Raven Rocks on your right at mile 6.9. Climb up and get southward views. Drop down from the outcrop and come to a junction at mile 7.1. Veer right and enter a hardwood forest, keeping a descent as the trail begins to turn more northerly. The trailbed here is less obvious; stay with the blue diamonds. Pointy Knob is off to your left. Cross South Fork Red Run and pick up an old railroad grade. The trail comes to a shelter at mile 8.3. This is a newer shelter, but has a similar design and serves as a good lunch spot. Leave the shelter and continue down the railroad grade, which stays on the hillside. At mile 9.5, the trail drops sharply to the right and makes the first of four crossings of South Fork Red Run. Look for bluffs alongside of and cascades on the creek.

Return to the grade and come to an open area, where you make a hard right, and cross Red Run. Continue up stream and climb the bank to arrive at Canaan Loop Road at mile 10.0. Turn left on Canaan Loop Road and follow it for 0.3 mile before coming to the Railroad Grade Trail on your right. As its name implies, it follows an old railroad grade and gently slabs the side of Canaan Mountain beneath a hardwood forest. The trail swings north and the forest becomes more evergreen until you come to a trail shelter, your second night's destination, at mile 11.5. This shelter is set in a deep valley and opens to the stream, which is your water source. A picnic table is a luxury here.

Start day three by continuing on the Railroad Grade Trail, climbing north. The trail leaves the bed where it levels out, avoiding mucky areas. The grade splits at mile 12.1 of your loop hike—take the right fork and continue east on the Plantation Trail. The trail here is very straight at times and passes a bog and a couple of streams, coming to the Lindy Run Trail (Forest Trail No. 109) at mile 13.5. Continue forward on the Plantation Trail. At times the trail bed is gravel, with large rocks lining the path. Cross Shays Run at mile 14.1, coming to Fire Trail No. 6 (Forest Trail No. 108) at mile 14.7. Keep east on the Plantation Trail. From this point forward you are retracing your steps from before, coming to the first night's shelter at mile 15.8 and keeping on the Plantation Trail. Come to

Fire Trail No. 3 (Forest Trail No. 104) at mile 17.4. Turn right, and ascend through the woods, completing your loop at mile 18.2.

Directions: From the town of Davis, drive south on State Road 32 for 3.3 miles to Canaan Loop Road. Turn right on Canaan Loop Road and follow it for 1.3 miles to the Fire Road No. 3 Trail (Forest Trail No. 104). The trail will be on your right; parking on your left.

Lower Otter Creek Wilderness

Scenery: ★★★★★   Difficulty: ★★★
Trail Condition: ★★★   Solitude: ★★
Children: ★
Distance: 3.2, 8.7, 8.6 miles each day
Hiking Time: 1:45, 5:45, 5:30 hours each day
Outstanding Features: wilderness stream, great views, campsites

This loop takes you through classic Appalachian mountain country. First, hike and camp on a mountain stream—Otter Creek—where clear waters crash over boulders, rest briefly in pools where secretive trout swim, and keep answering to gravity's pull. You, however, fight gravity and climb into the high country on Shavers Mountain to camp atop this mountain with a great view. Finally amble along Green Mountain, enjoying one more vista before dropping back down to Otter Creek.

Start your loop by leaving the parking area, and enter the woods on a gated forest road. Wind down to Dry Fork and cross this river's elaborate footbridge. Immediately turn right and follow Dry Fork downstream just a bit, coming to an Otter Creek Wilderness sign at 0.2 mile. Turn left, uphill, on a footpath and parallel Otter Creek upstream. Do not cross Otter Creek here. Pass a small waterfall dripping from the bluff to your left. Open up to a clearing and walk by the foundations of an old homesite. Come to the actual Otter Creek Wilderness boundary at 0.9 mile, at Coal Run. Trace a railroad grade upstream beneath a tall forest of tulip trees, which are present at lower elevations in the Central Appalachians. The elevation here is just over 1800 feet.

The railroad grade stays nearly level and straight, making for easy hiking. At mile 2.0, traverse an area where the railroad grade cuts through the hill. At mile 2.5, the trail becomes pinched in by a bluff on your left and the creek to your right. Make a sweeping turn south and come to a trail junction at mile 3.0. This junction, like all others in this wilderness, is marked by

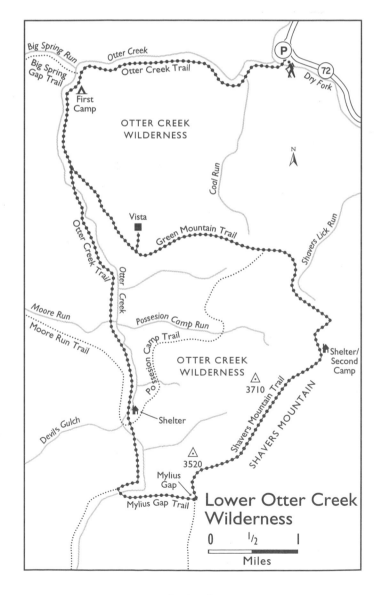

Lower Otter Creek Wilderness

rock cairns. Coming in from your right is the Big Spring Gap Trail. Stay forward on the Otter Creek Trail, which becomes pinched in once again. Then a flat by the creek opens up to your right at mile 3.2, which has campsites. This is your first night's destination.

Start day two by continuing on the Otter Creek Trail. This section of stream has many alluring swimming and fishing holes. It is dotted with big boulders good for sunning. At mile 4.1 of your loop hike, the Green Mountain Trail splits off to your left. This will be your return route. Keep forward and swing by a large clearing. Just past this clearing, cross Otter Creek onto a sandy beach. Keep heading upstream, rising far above the river. Work your way around a landslide area at mile 4.9. Look for a falls on Otter Creek at mile 5.2. Step over Moore Run at mile 6.1. Rhododendron crowds the pathway.

Pass some overhanging mossy bluffs at mile 6.8. The trail becomes washed out as you near the creek. Ford Otter Creek at mile 7.3, then come to the Otter Creek shelter. Keep forward, coming to a four-way trail junction at mile 7.5. Moore Run Trail leaves right, Possession Camp Trail leaves left. Stay forward on the Otter Creek Trail. Cross a side stream at mile 7.8. The trail then curves back to the right and crosses Otter Creek. Continue upstream, coming to another junction at mile 8.6. Turn left on the Mylius Trail, dropping down into a rhododendron thicket, then cross Otter Creek yet again.

Cross several tiny streambeds along the mild and shady upgrade. Come to Mylius Gap on Shavers Mountain at mile 9.5. There are several rock cairns here, marking the trails. Turn left, following the Shavers Mountain Trail north. Slab alongside the ridge for 0.6 mile. The footpath is much narrower than the railroad grades below. Once atop the ridge, walk northeasterly, undulating upward on an old woods road. Enter the first of many hemlock thickets at mile 10.9. This hemlock forest peaks out in an area of old growth trees at mile 11.3, where there is a huge hemlock just to the left of the trail and an old yellow birch. Come to a four-way trail junction at mile 11.9. To your right is the 0.1 mile trail to the Shavers Mountain shelter, your second night's destination. To your left is a 0.1 mile trail to a spring. Straight ahead is the continuation of the Shavers Mountain Trail. Turn right and head toward the shelter, which may or may not be here upon your arrival. The forest service is considering removing the two trail shelters currently in the Otter Creek Wilderness. There is a great view to the east of the Glady Fork valley and Middle Mountain from here. There are good campsites on the trail to the spring as well.

Start day three by continuing north on the Shavers Mountain Trail. Mostly descend for 0.5 mile and come to another junction. To your left is the beginning of the Green Mountain Trail, and the old Shavers Mountain Trail lies ahead. A sign here says, "Trail Abandoned." Turn sharply left on the Green Mountain Trail. The surprising path keeps changing, traversing open woods, bogs, thickets, rocky areas, and evergreen stands. Begin to descend at mile 13.3 and come to a clearing at mile 13.7. To your left is the Possession Camp Trail. Stay right, picking up a railroad grade and staying on the Green Mountain Trail. At mile 14.2, leave the grade and make a sharp left turn, then swing around a glade on your left. Walk a rocky downgrade beside a streambed and make an unexpected right turn at mile 14.8. Keep your eye peeled for a foot trail leading off to your right at mile 15.1. This trail leads 0.2 mile to a rocky vista. Here, you can overlook the Otter Creek valley. Take the extra time to enjoy this view.

Just after the side trail to the vista, the Green Mountain Trail begins to drop steeply into Otter Creek valley. The path is rocky. Pick up an old roadbed in a small flat at mile 15.6 and keep descending, coming to Otter Creek Trail at mile 16.4. You just dropped 1,100 feet in 1.3 miles. Turn right and begin retracing your steps downstream on Otter Creek Trail. Pass the Big Spring Gap Trail at mile 17.5. Continue down the valley, passing the wilderness boundary marker by Coal Run at mile 19.6. Cross Dry Fork on the elaborate footbridge at mile 20.3. Head up the gated road and come to the Otter Creek parking area, completing your loop at mile 20.5.

Directions: From downtown Parsons, head north on US 219 for 1.9 miles to West Virginia 72. Turn right on WV 72 and follow it 4.4 miles to the Otter Creek trailhead. This will be a signed right turn to the parking lot.

McGowan Mountain

Scenery: ★★★★	Difficulty: ★★★
Trail Condition: ★★★★	Solitude: ★★★
Children: ★★	

Distance: 1.9, 9.7, 7.5 miles each day
Hiking Time: 1:30, 6:00, 4:00 hours each day
Outstanding Features: wilderness setting, views

This hike loops the upper valley of Otter Creek within the Otter Creek Wilderness. Start an easy first day by dropping down the headwaters of Otter Creek, only to turn up Yellow Creek and camp near a meadow. Then climb up the headwaters of Yellow Creek and along McGowan Mountain before descending on the Moore Run Trail, where there are good views of a massive bog along the stream.

Drop down to Otter Creek, where there are fishing and swimming opportunities, then find solitude along the upper reaches of the Mylius Trail, where you'll spend your second night. Return along a lesser-used section of the Shavers Mountain Trail, where the hiking is challenging, before dropping back down to your point of origin.

Leave the Condon Run trailhead and follow the gated road to a footbridge. Cross Condon Run on the footbridge, enter a field and continue on the road. This road leads down to a limestone treatment plant constructed to reduce acidity in Otter Creek and to improve the fish habitat. Stay on the road for 0.2 mile, then turn left on the Otter Creek Trail, entering the wilderness. Follow an old roadbed, flanked by rhododendron.

Come alongside Otter Creek, then enter a clearing at 1.0 mile. An old railroad bridge abutment is alongside Otter Creek. Turn left, tracing the grade, and step over sandy Yellow Creek. Enter a hemlock wood, then come to the Yellow Creek Trail at 1.2 miles, marked by the rock cairns you'll see at all trail junctions. Turn left on the Yellow Creek Trail and make a moderate climb in a hemlock and rhododendron woods. At mile 1.8, intersect the McGowan Mountain Trail, coming in from your right. Keep forward, cross Yellow Creek, and come to a campsite in a stand of red pine at mile 1.9. This is your first night's destination. There are other campsites in the perimeter of the bog here.

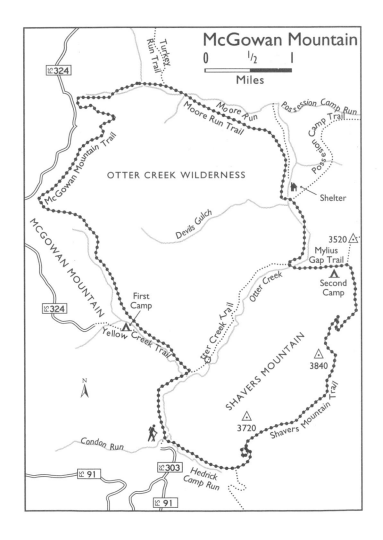

Start day two by returning to the McGowan Mountain Trail, turning left at mile 2.0 of your loop hike. Make a moderate climb among dense rhododendron. Pass an actual rail from the old railroad grade at mile 2.4. The climb soon begins in earnest, and spruce and hemlock begin to dominate the woodland. At mile 3.2, just past a small seep, the trail leaves the railbed and veers right. Be careful here, as the path is not as obvious as before. Irregularly ascend McGowan Mountain. Rhododendron is ever present. At mile 3.8, skirt between three house-sized boulders. Top out and begin an extended downgrade. In places, the rhododendron gives way to a maple-beech-birch forest complex with an open understory.

At mile 5.2, make a sudden and sharp downgrade between some boulders, coming to a roadbed. Turn right and follow the roadbed just a short distance, dropping left into more rhododendron, then come to the Moore Run Trail at mile 5.6. To your left a short distance is a spring branch. Turn right on the Moore Run Trail, descending to pick up a rail grade alongside the stream. Follow Moore Run and open into a big clearing at mile 5.9.

Reenter the woods, then come to a small glade. Turn sharply left here, and cross Moore Run at mile 6.2. Begin to swing around an immense bog, with flora similar to arctic bogs, on your right. Descend to the Turkey Run Trail at mile 6.8.

Stay forward on the Moore Run Trail in rhododendron. Pick up the railroad grade again in 0.1 mile. Cross a feeder stream, then Moore Run at mile 7.3. The rail grade now turns far away from Moore Run. The pathway is mostly easy, cutting through points of the ridge. There are numerous multi-trunked maple trees overhead. To your left are obscured views of the Otter Creek drainage.

Veer down and to the south along the ridgeside. Otter Creek becomes audible. At mile 9.6, the grade veers up to the right. Stay forward, then drop sharply left down to Otter Creek. Notice the big pool downstream. Cross Otter Creek and come to a trail junction at mile 9.7. Turn right, and follow the Otter Creek Trail upstream. There are numerous pools and cascades that invite exploration. Cross a side stream at mile 10.0. The trail then curves back to the right and crosses Otter Creek.

Continue upstream, coming to another junction at mile 10.8. Turn left on the Mylius Gap Trail, dropping down into a rhododendron thicket, then cross Otter Creek yet again. Cross several dry streambeds along the mild and shady upgrade. At mile 11.5, come to a small feeder stream of Otter Creek. Up to your right, on a flat, is a campsite. This is your second night's destination. This area offers much more solitude than the other campsites on Otter Creek. Fish, swim, and otherwise enjoy Otter Creek, then come up here to enjoy a quiet camping experience. There is a small glade on the far side of the feeder stream if you want to be in the sun.

Start day three by continuing up the Mylius Trail. Climb east up to Mylius Gap on Shavers Mountain at mile 11.7 of your loop hike. There are several rock cairns here, marking the trails. Turn right, following the Shavers Mountain Trail south. The forest here is mixed with drier species such as oak, interspersed with Fraser, magnolia, and hemlock. The climb begins innocently, and levels out, passing a property boundary marker at mile 12.4. Then begin switchbacking up Shavers Mountain. The climb eases up in an evergreen thicket at mile 13.3, then ascends moderately through the shady woods. Top out at mile 13.7; you just climbed nearly 700 feet.

Immediately lose elevation. There are obscured views off to your left of the Glady Fork valley and Middle Mountain. Turn away from the ridge, skirting a knob to your left. Begin to see more property markers also to your left. Pick up an old roadbed at mile 14.6. The trail makes an easy downgrade. Leave the roadbed, and drop off the side of the ridge at mile 15.4. Make four switchbacks downhill. Pick up another roadbed coming in from your right and intersect the Hedrick Camp Trail at mile 16.0. Stay forward

on the Hedrick Camp Trail. Come alongside this headwater of Otter Creek. Leave the old roadbed at mile
16.8, dropping off to the left into rhododendron.
Cross Otter Creek on a footbridge at mile 16.9. Enter a
hemlock wood and stay forward. Condon Run is on
your right and a meadow is on your left. Emerge onto
the closed forest road near the Condon Run trailhead
and turn left. Take a few steps back to the parking
area, completing your loop at mile 17.2.

Directions: From Elkins, drive east on US 33 for 11.5
miles to Stuart Memorial Drive, Forest Service Road
91, at Alpena Gap on Shavers Mountain. Turn left on
FS 91 and follow it for 1.1 miles to a junction. Stay forward at the junction, now on FS 303, and dead end at
the Condon Run trailhead in 0.4 mile.

Dolly Sods Wilderness

Scenery: ★★★★★	Difficulty: ★★★
Trail Condition: ★★★	Solitude: ★★
Children: ★★	

Distance: 2.4, 10.6, 6.4 miles each day
Hiking Time: 1:45, 5:15, 3:45 hours each day
Outstanding Features: great views, waterfalls, good
   campsites

Make this loop in the renowned Dolly Sods
Wilderness. This slice of the Monongahlea has nearly
everything: rocky vistas, open glades resembling the
western United States, thick spruce, northern hardwood forests, and a deep canyon cut by Red Creek. On
this loop, walk some high country and camp up high
by a great lookout, then swing west over Breathed
Mountain, and drop down Big Stonecoal Trail to camp
down in the Red Creek Canyon. Your final day climbs
back up. During World War II, Dolly Sods was a
bombing range, and there are still shells lying around.
If you see one, do not touch it! Mark the area, make a
map, and report it to a ranger station. Chances are,
however, you won't see one.

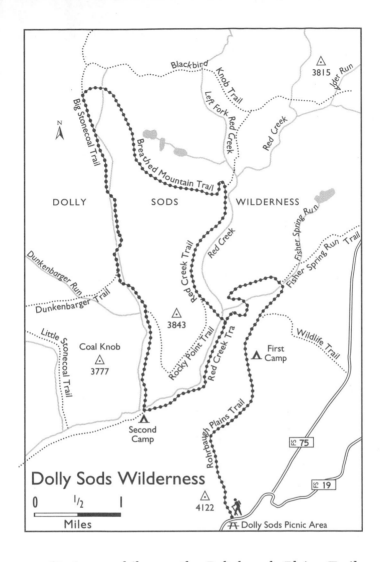

Dolly Sods Wilderness

0 ▐ 1/2 ▐ 1

Miles

Start your hike on the Rohrbough Plains Trail, Forest Trail No. 508, which begins just north of the Dolly Sods Picnic Area. Scramble up the roadbank and come to an elaborate trail board about the Dolly Sods. This trail starts as a footpath and is not the gated road just south of the picnic area. Enter a beech, cherry, and spruce forest lined with rhododendron. Begin to descend at 0.4 mile, crossing a railroad grade at 0.7 mile. A couple of tiny stream crossings precede skirting the edge of a glade at mile 1.2. You are now on an old railroad bed. Keep hiking northwesterly. The rocky trail seems elevated—this is the grade being raised over marshy areas. Rock cairns mark the rho-dodendron lined trail.

Cross the first significant stream at mile 2.3, which can easily be rock-hopped. At mile 2.4 on your left, a rock face offers good views, then the views improve as the outcrop extends farther from the forest. Relax, drop your pack, and find a campsite back in the woods near here. This is your first night's destination. You can enjoy the view of the Red Creek gorge below. Rocky Point on Breathed Mountain is just across the chasm.

Start day two by continuing north on the Rohrbaugh Plains Trail. Leave the outcrops, pass through a field, and follow an old road and a wide open walk. Watch for a pile of rocks to the left of the road, indicating a trail junction at mile 3.1 of your loop hike. Straight ahead, the road is now the Wildlife Trail. You turn left on the Rohrbaugh Plains Trail and follow an old railroad grade downhill. Descend and cross Fisher Spring Run at mile 3.4. Immediately enter a boulder field before coming to the junction with the Fisher Spring Run Trail, which intersects from your right by a pile of rocks at mile 3.5.

The main railroad grade is now the Fisher Spring Run Trail. Keep forward on the grade in the boulder-laden valley. Leave the grade at mile 3.9 and dive down to the left via switchbacks to cross Fisher Spring Run again. Work your way around a washed-out section of trail, ultimately keeping downstream. Red Creek is off to your right down a steep embankment. Come to a pile of cairns and another trail junction, while still high on the mountainside. Below you is a campsite. Take the trail leading to the campsite, which is the Red Creek Trail. Parallel Red Creek downstream just below a waterfall and big pool, and ford Red Creek. This is a nice spot to while away part of a day. Climb out of the flood-scoured creekbed, coming to another junction at mile 4.4 on the far side of Red Creek. The Rocky Point Trail goes left. You go right, upstream along Red Creek Trail. The valley floor is particularly attractive here, with mossy boulders beneath the yellow birch and hemlock. The trail leaves the valley at mile 4.6 and climbs steeply through a rhododendron thicket.

Cross one railroad grade, but pick up the second grade at mile 4.8. This provides a gentle ascent through a forest accentuated with rock outcrops and ferns everywhere. Come to the Breathed Mountain Trail at mile 6.0. Turn left here and climb steeply amid a boulder garden to top out on a grassy plateau at mile 6.3. The trail works across the plateau through clearings in dense spruce thickets, and areas where field and forest are mixed. Little rills meander toward the lowlands. Notice also planted red pines. Cross several small streams and mucky areas before coming to a grassy clearing and a junction with the Big Stonecoal Trail at mile 8.5.

Turn left on the Big Stonecoal Trail and immediately descend across a wet area on footlogs and stones. Make a couple of watery crossings. You are obviously following a railroad bed. Cross Big Stonecoal Run at mile 10.0. There is a wide open field with a great view to your right and a planting of red pine to your left. Wind your way through the red pine plantation. After this there are many open glades, woods, and small streams, crossing Big Stonecoal again at mile 10.8. Intersect the Dunkenbarger Trail, coming in on your right at mile 11.0. Stay forward on the Big Stonecoal Trail, quickly making another crossing, then stay on the grade as Big Stonecoal Run drops far off to your right.

Intersect the Rocky Point Trail at mile 11.6, which comes at you on the railroad grade. You, however, drop sharply right down a footpath, still on the Big Stonecoal Trail, and immediately passing a side trail to a rock outcrop with a view of a falls on Big Stonecoal Run. The stream is far below, but the noisy watercourse is clearly audible on the mountainside. Keep dropping and pick up another grade. At mile 12.5, work around a slide that has eroded the railroad grade. Drop steeply down just before coming to Red Creek. At mile 12.9, the trail seemingly ends in a bluff. Make your way down to the water and make the wet booted ford above the confluence of Big Stonecoal and Red creeks, coming to the Red Creek Trail and a flat with many campsites at mile 13.0. This is your second night's destination.

Start day three by heading upstream on the Red Creek Trail. Follow a railroad grade up for 0.2 mile, watching for a footpath that splinters off to the right, away from the grade. Climb up along the mountain-side, crossing a seep, and then a stream at mile 13.4 of your loop hike. You are way above the river before dropping down to a side stream at mile 13.9. Look for a side trail dropping down to a falls on this stream. Keep on the Red Creek Trail, coming to a junction with the Fisher Spring Run Trail at mile 14.7. From this point forward you are retracing your steps, coming to the Rohrbaugh Plains Trail at mile 15.9, the Wildlife Trail at mile 16.3, and the first night's camp by the outcrop at mile 17.0. Get one more view before returning to the Dolly Sods Picnic Area at mile 19.4 and completing your loop.

Directions: From Petersburg, drive south on West Virginia 28 for 8.5 miles to Jordan Run Road (CR 28/7). Turn right on Jordan Run Road and follow it for 1.0 mile to Forest Service Road 19, which will be on your left. Turn left on FS 19 and follow it for 6.0 miles to the junction with FS 75. Stay left on FS 19 and drive 1.2 miles to the Dolly Sods Picnic Area.

Spruce Knob-
Laurel Fork Area

Big Run/Leading Ridge

Scenery: ★★★★   Difficulty: ★★
Trail Condition: ★★★★★   Solitude: ★★★
Children: ★★★
Distance: 1.9, 3.9, 5.6 miles each day
Hiking Time: 1:30, 2:45, 3:45 each day
Outstanding Features: meadows, good campsites,
    wildlife clearings

This loop traverses the lesser-used west side of the Seneca Creek Backcountry. Though this area rivals the eastern side of the hiking area in overall beauty, the crowds stay away from here because it lacks specific attractive features such as falls or vistas. However, make this loop if you like intimate stream valleys, good campsites, and solitude. Head up Big Run to a meadow-laden upper valley to spend your first night. Then walk the North Prong Trail, one of the prettiest paths in the Seneca Creek Backcountry, to the ridge-line and the Allegheny Mountain Trail, where you will spend your second night up high, by a wildlife clearing. Your final day is on the Leading Ridge Trail, where numerous wildlife clearings increase your chances of spotting deer and other animals. The daily mileages are short, which avails plenty of time for exploring or lazing around the campsite.

Leave the Big Run parking area on the Big Run Trail and cross Gandy Creek on an arched footbridge. You can see Big Run coming in across Gandy Creek from the bridge. Climb away from Gandy Creek, following the blue diamonds across an old road, and enter a field. Leave the field and reenter the woods at 0.2 mile. On a railroad grade, begin to parallel Big Run in a forest primarily of northern hardwoods. Work your way through irregular rockbeds of stream over-flow. Step over Big Run at 0.5 mile and 0.8 mile. Soon after the second crossing, look for a bridge abutment

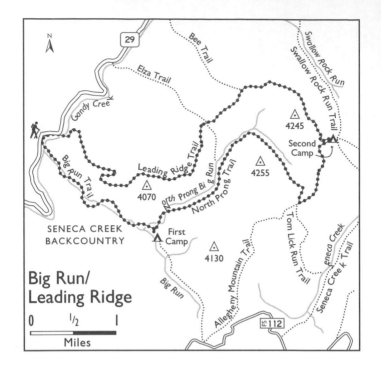

of rock near a dry stream meander. Cross Big Run again at 0.9 mile into a cleared area. The valley becomes forested again, as the trail crosses Big Run twice in succession at mile 1.2, in an area frequently subject to flooding. Cross Big Run a final time at mile 1.5. Then, at mile 1.6, step over North Prong and come to a trail junction in a meadow. Turn right at the junction, still on the Big Run Trail, pass an old apple tree, and enter the woods. There is a planting of red pines on your right. Climb along the edge of the valley. Begin looking for a grassy flat off to your right, beneath some yellow birch, cherry, and maple. Here in the flat, at mile 1.9, is your first night's destination. Water is available from the nearby creek. Take time to explore the valley upstream from here, as there are large clearings, beaver dams, and good ridgeline views.

Start day two by returning 0.3 mile to the Big Run-North Prong Trail junction. At mile 2.2 of your loop hike, turn right on the North Prong Trail. Begin walking up the small, scenic valley, crossing North Prong three times. Skirt a clearing and red pine plantation where a feeder stream comes in from your right.

The valley narrows and closes. Cross North Prong twice more before intersecting the Elza Trail at mile 3.4. Stay forward on North Prong Trail. Watch for beaver dams as the valley opens up, and come to a large meadow at mile 4.1. Stay along the right edge of this scenic clearing, and ascend steadily through woodland to a high point and another clearing. Stay left in this clearing to descend to yet another clearing and some red pines at mile 4.9. Here is the junction with the ridge running Allegheny Mountain Trail.

Turn left on the Allegheny Mountain Trail, heading north. Watch for a wildlife clearing off to your left at mile 5.0. Descend past the Leading Ridge Trail at mile 5.4. This will be your return route. Beyond this junction, at mile 5.6, pass a wildlife pond and spring on your right. Keep dropping and come to another trail junction at mile 5.8. On your right is a sloped clearing. The Swallow Rock Run Trail drops off both sides of the ridge. Just to your left, in the woods, is a campsite. This is your second night's destination. Water can be had from either the spring back up the Allegheny Mountain Trail, or a spring 0.3 mile down the Swallow Rock Run Trail, away from the sloped clearing. If you have the time and energy, drop a mile down the Swallow Rock Run Trail toward the clearing to Seneca Creek. From here it is another 2.7 miles downstream to Upper Seneca Falls. Then you can return to this side of the Seneca Creek Backcountry.

Start day three by backtracking 0.4 mile up the Allegheny Mountain Trail, intersecting the Leading Ridge Trail at mile 6.2 of your loop hike. Turn right on the Leading Ridge Trail and stay right while climbing up the sloped wildlife clearing. The wide grassy path makes for easy hiking and good footing, which facilitates your enjoyment of the attractive northern hardwood forest. The understory is light, making wildlife easier to observe. And you may see deer or turkeys on this path, which enjoy the food plots of the clearings and also the ponds, which make water easier to obtain. The trail curves from north to west to south to west while making its way back to Gandy Creek. First head north, passing wildlife clearings at miles 6.6, 7.3, and 7.8. The Bee Trail comes in from your right at this last clearing. Stay forward and climb, now heading southerly.

Pass another clearing at mile 8.2, then drop down to intersect the Elza Trail at mile 8.5. Stay forward on the Leading Ridge Trail and begin a half mile climb to a high point. There are ridgeline views to your left while ascending. From here, it is literally all downhill. Head through more wildlife clearings, watching for the blue diamond trail markers.

At mile 10.1, stay right at an obvious fork in the trail, then swing around to the head of Camp Seven Hollow (The left fork leads to another wildlife clearing). Drop down the tiny valley strewn with large boulders, now heading westerly. Pass through a rhododendron thicket at mile 10.9. Veer south down to Gandy Creek and come to an arched footbridge over the stream. Cross the footbridge and emerge onto County Road 29 at mile 11.1. Turn left on the gravel road and come to the Big Run parking area, completing your loop at mile 11.4.

Directions: From the town of Seneca Rocks, head south on US 33 for 13 miles to Briery Gap Road. Turn right on Briery Gap Road and follow it up for 2.5 miles to Forest Service Road 112. Turn right on FS 112 and head up 13.2 miles to FS 1. Turn right on FS 1 and follow it 4.1 miles to County Road 29. Stay right and follow CR 29 for 2.4 miles to a parking area on your right. The Big Run Trail starts here.

Seneca Creek/High Meadows

Scenery: ★★★★★   Difficulty: ★★
Trail Condition: ★★   Solitude: ★★★
Children: ★★★
Distance: 3.2, 4.4, 5.9 miles each day
Hiking Time: 1:45, 3:15, 3:15 hours each day
Outstanding Features: waterfalls, meadows, great vistas

This loop traverses some of the most spectacular scenery in the Seneca Creek Backcountry. First, walk down Seneca Creek, with its meadows, waterfalls, and trout fishing opportunities, to stay at Judy Springs, a walk-in campground. Continue down Seneca Creek to the Upper Falls of Seneca. Head into the uplands on the High Meadows Trail, which offers incredible vistas, then spend your second night on the edge of a meadow with good views. Complete your loop on an old logging grade that offers easy but soggy trekking. The days are fairly short, which allows extra time to explore the landscape around you, minus the pack.

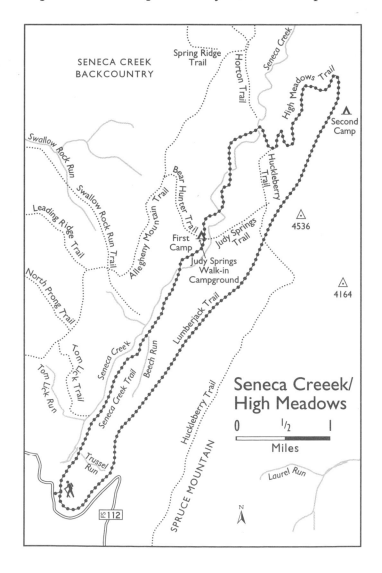

Start your hike by leaving Forest Service Road 112, and following the Seneca Creek Trail down the valley of Seneca Creek. The path is partially canopied by spruce and hardwoods. Step over Trussel Run at 0.4 mile, and intersect the Tom Lick Trail at 0.9 mile. Stay forward on the Seneca Creek Trail. The path is sometimes open and sometimes lined with spruce. The valley to your left has many meadows and occasional beaver dams. Numerous feeder streams flow in from Spruce Mountain to your right. Cross Beech Run at mile 1.9. Wind through some hardwoods and pass the Swallow Rock Trail at mile 2.1.

Keep heading down the valley and cross Seneca Creek at mile 2.7. Look for bluffs and waterfalls across the watercourse just before arriving at the Judy Springs Walk-In Campground at mile 3.2. This is your first night's destination. There are many shaded campsites in the perimeter of the meadow. Just across the footbridge to your right is the short trail to Judy Springs.

Start day two by heading down Seneca Creek through the meadow, shortly passing the Bear Hunter Trail. Bend to the right and look for two more falls coming into Seneca Creek on the far side of the stream. Make a wet ford of Seneca Creek at mile 3.6 of your loop hike. Just past the ford look for two large falls on Seneca Creek. Make another ford at mile 4.1. Keep down the valley of birch, beech, and maple.

Come to a meadow at mile 4.6. Look for another pair of side falls to your right, before coming to the final ford of Seneca Creek at mile 4.9. Be careful here, as the ford is just above a six-foot cascade. Just ahead is the Huckleberry Trail, leaving to your right. Continue just a bit farther and come to the Upper Falls of Seneca. Here, Seneca Creek drops over 30 feet into a pool. A trail leads down to the pool. Return to the Huckleberry Trail.

Climb steeply 100 feet up to an old logging grade and make a sharp right. Swing past a cascading falls of a side stream and cross this watercourse at mile 5.0. Pick up another logging grade and begin walking upstream along Seneca Creek. Climb up a second side stream and step over this stream at mile 5.2. Make an arduous ascent along the creek to emerge onto a sloped meadow. Stay to the right of the stream in this meadow, briefly reenter the woods, and come to a trail junction at mile 5.4. Turn left on the High Meadows Trail. Cross the stream you've been following and emerge onto a wide open sloped meadow with incredible views of the Seneca Creek valley and surrounding mountains. Watch for plastic shafts topped with blue diamonds marking the route through the meadows here.

Make a sharp right at mile 5.5 and head uphill, slabbing to your left. In the summer there will be cattle grazing in the meadows. The sloping meadow gives way to a wooded stream valley at mile 5.7. Pass a couple of rills and emerge onto another meadow at mile 5.8. Keep angling uphill, pass through a patch of woods, and come to a third meadow at mile 6.0. Enter the woods yet again, come to an obvious railbed, and then turn left. The grade makes a level path through the rocky woods.

Open onto another meadow at mile 6.6. Immediately leave the grade you have been following, veering steeply up and to the right. Don't forget to look back for more good views. Level onto a grassy flat just before more woods. Turn left onto an old woods road. Cross several spring seeps at mile 7.3. Watch for the remains of an old wire fence to your left, just before taking a sharp right-hand turn at mile 7.5.

You are now on the Lumberjack Trail. To your left is an attractive meadow. Continue 0.1 mile farther and look for a path leading up and to the left toward the meadow. Look around this area for campsites underneath the trees on the perimeter of the broken meadow. This is your second night's destination. Water can be had back at the last spring seep on the High Meadows Trail. This is a great place to while away a summer or fall afternoon.

Start day three by returning to the Lumberjack Trail. Head south along the west slope of Spruce Mountain. The old railroad grade is very level but is mucky in places, due to seeps coming down from Spruce Mountain. Occasionally detour around very wet spots in the grade. Plan to get your boots muddy here. You'll be around 4,000 feet up in a forest of northern hardwoods and spruce.

Pass a small meadow at mile 8.9. Make a moderate descent down to a trail junction at mile 9.6. Keep forward on the Lumberjack Trail, passing more seeps. At mile 10.2, pass the remains of stone bridge abutments, relics from the logging days. Look for other stonework along the grade. The mountainside has become less steep by the time you skirt the right edge of a meadow at mile 11.4. Leave the rail grade and walk through a smaller meadow to avoid a mucky area at mile 12.5. Bisect a few more streamlets before stepping over a rock vehicle barrier to arrive at Forest Service Road 112 at mile 13.0. Turn right on FS 112 and head mostly downhill around a curve, arriving at the Seneca Creek parking area at mile 13.5, completing your loop.

Directions: From the town of Seneca Rocks, head south on US 33 for 13 miles to Briery Gap Road. Turn right on Briery Gap Road and follow it up for 2.5 miles to Forest Service Road 112. Turn right on FS 112 and head up 11.3 miles to the Seneca Creek trailhead, which will be on your right.

Cranberry Area

Cranberry Backcountry

Scenery: ★★★★	Difficulty: ★★★
Trail Condition: ★★★★	Solitude: ★★★
Children: ★★	
Distance: 5.0, 7.8, 7.6 miles each day	
Hiking Time: 2:45, 4:45, 4:45 hours each day	
Outstanding Features: good fishing, solitude on North-South Trail, some views	

This loop rambles through the Monongahela's historic Cranberry Backcountry, a primitive area that campers and hikers have been enjoying since the inception of the national forest. Start your loop by winding along the Cranberry River, one of West Virginia's outstanding fisheries, to a trail shelter, where you'll spend your first night. The walk thus far is easy and remains that way for a few more miles, until you turn up Birchlog Run and head into the highlands and the North-South Trail. Make your second night's camp at a gap near the Little Fork Trail. Your final day takes you through a sparsely-used section of the North-South Trail, back down to the Cranberry River. Other

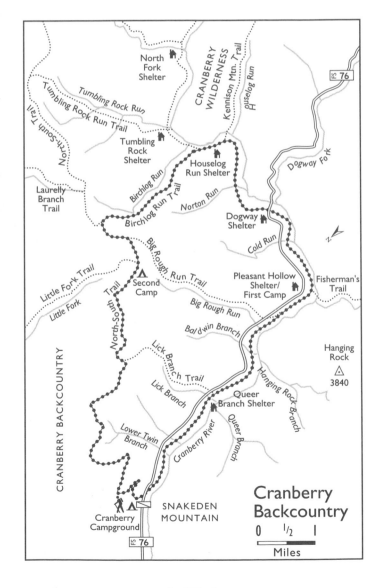

recreationalists will be seen on the Cranberry River, but after that you should enjoy solitude aplenty.

Start your hike by walking around the gate blocking all but official vehicular traffic on Forest Service Road 76. Cranberry River is on your right as you immediately pass the North-South Trail, which will be your return route. Walk up the moderately graded gravel road, which allows more views of the hardwood forest. Many old seeded roads spur from the main route. Sporadic clearings begin to appear. Come to Lower Twin Branch at 0.9 mile; watch for beaver dams on your right. Look for bridge pilings crossing the Cranberry River to your right at mile 1.2. Large erosion-preventing boulders have been placed along the riverbank where the road meets the river. Come to the Queer Branch Shelter at mile 2.0. Keep forward, heading southerly, and pass the Lick Branch Trail on your left in 0.3 mile. Notice the pretty cascade just up Lick Branch. Just before coming to Baldwin Branch at mile 3.6, there is a gnarled oak tree right by the river, which has survived many floods in its day. The Rough Run Trail comes in on your left at mile 4.0. Past this, the route climbs more steeply and rises far above the Cranberry River. Intersect the Fisherman's Trail on your right, and shortly come to the Pleasant Hollow Shelter at mile 5.0. This is your first night's destination. The shelter overlooks the Cranberry River and a steep bluff across the waterway. There are many other suitable campsites in the area. The pools and runs of the Cranberry and nearby Dogway Fork make for numerous angling opportunities.

Start day two by continuing up FS 76, which turns easterly, immediately passing a large clearing on your right. Cross Cold Run at mile 6.0 of your loop hike. This section of road has many open areas that can be steamy on a summer day; they also afford fine ridgeline vistas of the Cranberry Backcountry. At mile 6.8, come to the Dogway Shelter on your right. Stay left here, now on closed FS 102. Continue to parallel the Cranberry River. Notice signs explaining catch and release fishing regulations. Pass Norton Run at mile 7.5. Shortly beyond this, red spruce and yellow birch, cooler situation trees, begin to appear. The Kennison Mountain Trail splits off to your right at mile 8.4. Immediately swing by a clearing, then come to the Houselog Run Shelter. This pretty area makes a good lunch or break spot.

Keep forward up the road at a mild grade and come to Birchlog Run Trail at mile 9.3. Fill your water bottles here, as aqua becomes more scanty up high. Turn left through a mostly clear area up the left bank of the stream. Soon turn away from the stream, and begin a series of sharp climbs, broken by easier stretches. After the first sharp climb, look for a huge house-sized boulder in the hollow to your right.

This trail was rerouted in the late 1990s and stays far above the Birchlog Run. The sloping terrain levels out in a flat of spruce, hemlock, and hardwoods. Swing left around a side hollow of Birchlog Run and cross a flowing streamlet at mile 10.7. Work your way back into the main hollow of Birchlog Run, and keep climbing to intersect the North-South Trail at mile 11.7. Turn left on the North-South Trail and begin walking amid hardwoods, beginning a brief climb in 0.2 mile. After a moderate descent, intersect the Big Rough Run Trail at mile 12.3, which leaves left toward the Cranberry River. You veer right, staying on the North-South Trail. The open path stays mostly level, through a forest of northern hardwoods such as cherry and beech. The trail drops a bit near some boulders just before arriving at the Little Fork Trail in a gap, at mile 12.8. Just past this gap is a campsite on your right. This is your second night's destination. Water is available down the Little Fork Trail. Level campsites with water-access are few and far between on the North-South Trail, so appreciate this spot.

Start day three by continuing on the North-South Trail. Climb up a knob between many boulders at mile 13.4 of your loop hike. The climb is moderated by a switchback. Top out in a shaded boulder and fern field. The treadway remains rocky while undulating along the ridgetop. Climb again at mile 14.3, soon passing a gnarly battle-scarred sugar maple on trail left. Intersect the Lick Branch Trail at mile 15.6, which leaves downhill to your left. You turn right, ascending slightly on the North-South Trail. Pass through many level sections, where the path may be mucky. At mile 16.8, the trail turns sharply left and descends to a gap. Pass a hunter's camp in a clearing off to your left at mile 17.2. There is a small stream here, if you need water. Continue along the ridge and enter a young forest of many pin cherry trees. An old jeep road comes in from your left.

Swing right and drop down past a wildlife clearing off to your left at mile 17.8. Pay close attention here, as the trail follows the Jeep road just a short distance into an open area at mile 18.0. The Jeep road continues forward. You follow the Jeep road just a few yards as it goes uphill, before you take an abrupt left at a trail sign that may be obscured by grass. The Jeep road continues forward. On the foot trail that has turned left, there are blue diamond markers in the woods indicating your direction. Enter the woods and cross the headwater of Lower Twin Branch three times, keeping downstream. The trail is now rooty and rocky. Pass near a huge hemlock tree at mile 18.6, just before picking up an old grade. Follow the grade a short distance and make an abrupt left across a mossy boulder field and streambed.

The trail meanders down a ridge before making a series of switchbacks that take you down the side of the ridge deep into the Cranberry River valley. This foot trail is narrow and its light use makes it harder to find than other portions of the North-South Trail. The river becomes audible, and FS 76 is visible down below before you intersect it. Turn right and walk a few steps back to the parking area, completing your loop at mile 20.4.

Directions: From Richwood, drive east on WV 39/55 for 0.5 mile to Cranberry Road (County Road 76) Turn left on Cranberry Road and follow it for nearly 3.0 miles to an intersection. Forest Service Road 76 veers left and is the only gravel road at this intersection. Follow FS 76 for 9.0 miles just past Cranberry Campground, where the road dead ends. Start your hike at the dead end on gated FS 76.

Middle Fork

Scenery: ★★★★　　　　Difficulty: ★★★
Trail Condition: ★★★　　Solitude: ★★★
Children: ★★
Distance: 2.4, 7.0, 10.8 miles each day
Hiking Time: 1:30, 4:00, 6:15 hours each day
Outstanding Features: waterfall, wilderness setting, diverse woods

This loop lies entirely within the Cranberry Wilderness. Work your way up the Middle Fork Cranberry River in a valley that has that everywhere-you-look beauty, starting in a forest of sycamore and tulip trees that are lesser seen in the Monongahela. Spend your first night along Big Beechy Run and a falls. Northern hardwoods become more prevalent farther up the valley, where the shady Middle Fork tumbles over big boulders. There are numerous swimming and fishing holes up here. Spend your second night on the upper reaches of Middle Fork at 4,000 feet. Enjoy your final day with a lighter pack, tramping through the high country spruce forests along Big Beechy Trail before dropping back down to the Middle Fork. For a more strenuous second day and easier third day, you can reverse your loop, making for an 8.3 mile second day and 9.4 mile third day, but Big Beechy Trail will be an uphill pull before looping back around to the Middle Fork. Your first day will remain the same. The climb is more gentle in the order described in this book.

Start this hike at Three Forks. Leave the parking area and immediately walk over a stream meander of the Middle Fork. Take a few steps into a clearing and come to the Little Fork Trail, which leaves to the right. Continue forward on the Middle Fork Trail, which fol-

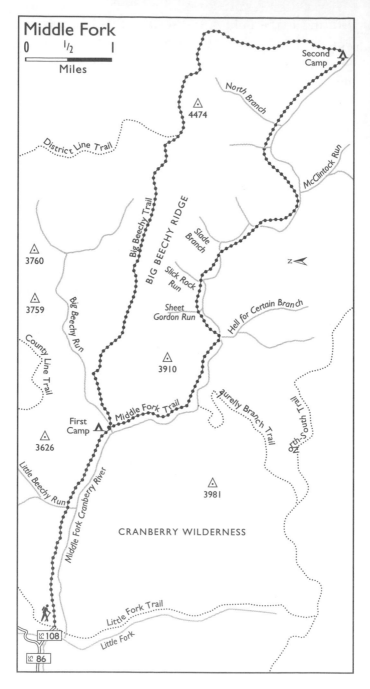

Middle Fork

0   ¹/₂   1
Miles

lows an old roadbed and railroad grade. Leave the clearing then pass a trailside kiosk on your left.

Even though you are headed upstream, the elevation change is nearly imperceptible. Enter a fast disappearing clearing at mile 0.4 and continue beneath a woodland of tulip trees, sycamore, sugar maple, and hemlock. County Line Ridge rises sharply to your left. Cross a concrete culvert over a streambed at mile 1.4, then saddle up alongside the Middle Fork. The trail becomes pinched in by a bluff on your left and the Middle Fork on your right. Piled logs and debris in the river indicate the flooding potential of this usually clear mountain stream where trout are often visible in pools below.

The former roadbed you are walking on often traces a railroad grade leftover from the logging days. Come to Big Beechy Run at mile 2.4. This is your first night's destination. Big Beechy Run Falls is just below the stream crossing. Just a few feet below the falls, Big Beechy Run merges with the Middle Fork to form a nice swimming hole. There are several spots in the vicinity that make for suitable campsites. More solitude can be found up Big Beechy Run.

Start day two by crossing Big Beechy Run. The Big Beechy Trail comes in from your left. This will be your return route. Stay forward on the Middle Fork Trail. Look to your right where the old railroad grade crossed Big Beechy Run just below the falls. Soon merge with the grade. The treadway steepens just a bit. Big Beechy Ridge is on your left, as you pass through a some rhododendron. At times the trail lies just by the stream and other times along wooded flats with Middle Fork in the distance. Look for a huge pile of rocks on your right at mile 3.4 of your loop hike. Come to a trail junction at mile 3.8. To your right, the Laurelly Branch Trail crosses Middle Fork. Stay left on the Middle Fork Trail, climbing to a point where an old railroad grade comes from your left before descending back to the river.

At mile 4.3, pass a very conspicuous rectangular boulder directly on the trail. The valley becomes more attractive with alternating bluffs and hollows. Make your first crossing of Middle Fork at mile 5.4. This can be rock-hopped at most times of the year. The path becomes very rough where the trailbed has become washed out. Pass through a few small clearings before crossing Middle Fork again at mile 6.1. The trail then climbs far above the stream before merging with the waterway again. Cross a meander of the Middle Fork twice at mile 6.9. There are more beech, yellow birch, and cherry trees as you gain elevation. Step over an unnamed branch coming in from trail left at mile 7.4, then cross over North Branch 0.3 mile farther. Enter a rhododendron tunnel to emerge at a glade. The trail steepens a little more as you skirt another small glade at mile 8.2. Red spruce begins to line the way. Work your way across more washed out areas. The trail makes a sharp turn to the left at mile 9.4. At the turn, look for a campsite on your right in a spruce flat. This is your second night's destination. If this campsite is occupied by some chance, backtrack just a short distance to another campsite across the stream.

Start day three by heading up the Middle Fork Trail. Fill your water bottles before you leave, as there is none regularly available for several miles. Climb a bit and come to a clearing and trail junction at mile 9.8 of your loop hike. Coming in from the right is the North Fork Trail. Keep forward on the roadbed, now heading northerly on the North Fork Trail.

The North Fork Trail makes a very level, pleasant walk. Small spruce line the path with bigger trees overhead on the partially canopied forest. Pass a large field on your left at mile 10.8. Just pass this clearing on your left is the Big Beechy Trail. Take this foot trail, which leaves the roadbed and skirts the right edge of the meadow. Begin to stairstep up to the ridge into a classic spruce woodland, where moss rocks carpet the forest floor and evergreens crowd out the sun.

At mile 11.9, the trail makes a sharp left and begins descending for a bit. Enter a rhododendron thicket, then a boulder-strewn forest where spruce grow atop the big rocks. Come to the District Line Trail at mile 13.0. Stay forward on the Big Beechy Trail, descending from the junction. Stay primarily on the right side of the ridge. Roots and rocks on the narrow treadway make for slower going than before.

In spots, hemlock and northern hardwoods predominate on the ridge. Drop down into an obvious gap at mile 14.6 where there is a campsite on your right. Slab around the left side of a knob and enter a rhododendron-hemlock thicket. Continue stairstepping down the ridge, dropping steeply at mile 16.2, and passing below large rock bluffs to your left. The spruce trees have been left behind.

Pick up an old railroad grade at mile 16.6, crossing over a spring on the remains of a wood bridge. Leave the grade in 0.2 mile, dropping off to your right. The narrow path slabs down the north side of the ridge and comes to the Middle Fork Trail at mile 17.8. Turn right, cross Big Beechy Run, and retrace your steps 2.4 miles back down Middle Fork Trail, completing your loop at mile 20.2.

Directions: From the Cranberry Visitor Center, 23 miles east of Richwood on WV 39/55, head north on WV 150, Highlands Scenic Highway, for 13.3 miles to Forest Service Road 86. Turn left on FS 86 and follow it for 11.5 miles to FS 108, just before the bridge over the Williams River. Turn left on FS 108 and follow it for 0.5 mile to dead-end at the Three Forks Area. The Middle Fork Trail starts at the far end of the parking area.

North-South

Scenery: ★★★★
Difficulty: ★★
Trail Condition: ★★★★
Solitude: ★★★
Children: ★★
Distance: 5.0, 7.7, 3.4 miles each day
Hiking Time: 3:15, 5:00, 2:15 hours each day
Outstanding Features: highland spruce forest, attractive mountain valley, good campsites.

This loop takes you into the heart of the Cranberry Wilderness. Leave the Highlands Scenic Highway and traverse the spruce woodlands of the high country and enjoy some ridgetop camping. Drop down Tumbling Rock Run and trace the Cranberry River. Then work your way up the extremely scenic North Fork

Cranberry River and do some streamside camping in a lovely spot. Your final day is uphill back to the Highlands Scenic Highway. None of the days are very long, and your uphill day is the shortest.

Leave the scenic highway at 4,500 feet and immediately step into the forest on the North-South Trail, which actually heads primarily east-west. Veer left, and pass a clearing and a trailside kiosk on your left. Keep west through a spruce flat with rocky, rooty footing. Pick up an old roadbed and intersect the North Fork Trail at mile 0.4. The portion of the North Fork Trail to your left will be part of your return route. Keep forward on the North-South Trail. Hundreds of small spruce grow below the taller evergreens overhead. Walk along the ridge, as rhododendron increase in number.

Come to a muddy section at 0.9 mile. Rocks have been placed on the trail for easier passage. In some places, the trail passes beneath open spruce woods and in other places rhododendron and laurel crowd the walkway. There will almost surely be some blown-down trees to work around at points. At mile 2.2, more hardwoods begin to appear on the ridgetop. Of note are yellow birch, cherry, and beech. The trail veers left at mile 2.9 and crosses an old road that is becoming overgrown. The treadway becomes narrower and begins to undulate. Deciduous trees are now in the majority. Swing around the left side of a knob at mile 3.9, then pass through a boulder field in a broken forest. Descend into a gap, with a grassy area to your left. Make a couple of more ups and downs, with the final drop to Tumbling Rock Trail traversing rocky woods. Intersect the Tumbling Rock Trail at mile 5.0.

There is a gap just beyond this intersection. This is your first night's destination. The campsite lies in a hardwood forest accentuated with hemlock trees. Water can be had at wet weather springs on either side of the gap, or by walking a good piece down the Tumbling Rock Trail in very dry times.

Start day two by returning to the Tumbling Rock Trail. Begin descending down Tumbling Rock Trail

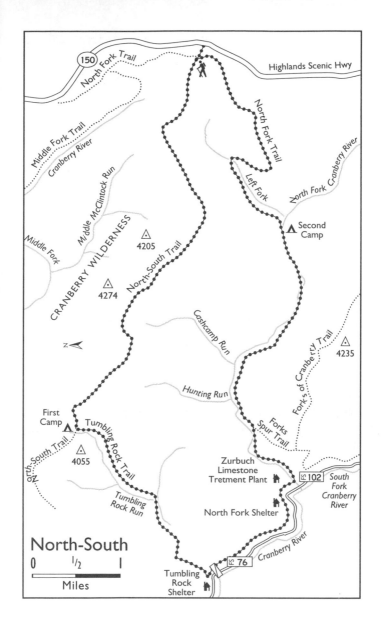

North-South

0   1/2   1

Miles

and pick up an old grade. Enter a wide flat at mile 5.3 of your loop hike. A feeder fork of Tumbling Rock Run comes in from the left. Here, the trail and creek beds merge in spots, making for messy passage. Notice the railroad ties imbedded in the grade at your feet. The main stream drops far below to your right, and feeder branches cut across the grade. Drop off the grade you've been following at mile 5.7 and keep descending. Pass through a flat with metal relics, indicating habitation. Feeder branches join here, making a full-fledged waterway.

Keep down the valley and cross Tumbling Rock Run at mile 6.1. Leave the grade; you are now following a footpath 100 or more feet above the stream. Swing back to the right and drop down to the side branch of Tumbling Creek at mile 6.7. Step across the stream that is coming in from your right and climb up to a well-graded footpath which leads toward Cranberry River. The trail hugs the mountainside and makes a sharp switchback left at an old road, then comes to the Cranberry River at mile 7.5. You have just left the Cranberry Wilderness. Intersect closed Forest Service Road 76. Only official vehicles are allowed passage on this route. Turn left up the forest road and cross Tumbling Rock Run on a road bridge. Parallel the Cranberry River upstream. The roadside is alternately field and forest. At times the road passes directly alongside the Cranberry River. Pass the North Fork trail shelter on your right at mile 9.1. Cross North Fork on a road bridge and come to the North Fork Trail at mile 9.2. Turn left on the road/trail and come to the Zurbuch Limestone Treatment Plant. Limestone is used to reduce acidity in the Cranberry River, making it better trout habitat. Stay to the right of the plant and pass a fine spring on your right.

Soon reenter the Cranberry Wilderness. You are walking streamside on an old road up the North Fork Cranberry River. Pass the Forks Spur Trail on your right at mile 9.8, which leads south to the Forks of Cranberry Trail. The North Fork Trail begins to ascend as it is pinched in by the ridge on your right and river to your left. Come to a clear area with views of the ridge you were walking yesterday. Large hemlock-rhododendron flats come between the trail and river in places. There is a clearing across the river at mile 10.8. Passage is easy where the trail is grassy, but at times crowded stands of red spruce make the going tough. Stay forward on the North Fork Trail and come to bridge abutments at mile 11.4. Here, you must rock-hop the North Fork.

Briefly pick up the road, then turn sharply left on a foot trail that swings uphill then upstream. The path is rooty and rocky. Return to the roadbed in 0.3 mile. Continue up the pretty valley, passing through more spruce thickets. Come to an obvious junction of old roads at mile 12.7. The road to your right leads slightly downhill to a flat and a campsite. This is your second night's destination. Near the campsite is the confluence of the North Fork and Left Fork of the Cranberry River. There is a small wading pool here. A wildlife clearing of several acres lies alongside North Fork near the campsite. These attributes make this an ideal camping spot.

Start day three by returning to the North Fork Trail. Head uphill on the old roadbed, now paralleling the Left Fork Cranberry River. Pass through one more spruce thicket and step over the Left Fork, at mile 13.4 of your loop hike. Turn back to the southwest, moderately ascending out of the valley. The trail bed is mostly open and mostly grass. At mile 13.7, walk through a muddy area created by a spring coming in from your left. Immediately come to rock cairns that signal a sharp turn to your left. Turn acutely left up to the grade your were just on (the grade made a switchback). Keep ascending, passing a streambed coming in from your right from beneath a big boulder at mile 14.0. Spruce begin to increase in number as your climb up the west flank of Black Mountain continues. Make your way through one more spruce thicket before emerging onto a grassy path and intersecting the North-South Trail at mile 15.7. Turn right and head east on the North-South Trail, retracing your steps for 0.4 mile, and completing your loop at mile 16.1.

Directions: From the Cranberry Visitor Center, 23 miles east of Richwood on WV 39/55, head north on WV 150, Highlands Scenic Highway, for 8.6 miles to the North-South Trail, which will be on your left.

Tea Creek Backcountry

Scenery: ★★★★   Difficulty: ★★★
Trail Condition: ★★★★   Solitude: ★★★
Children: ★★
Distance: 2.8, 9.2, 8.4 miles each day
Hiking Time: 2:00, 6:00, 5:30 hours each day
Outstanding Features: well marked trails, backcountry
    shelters, views

This is a great break-in hike for first-time National Forest backpackers or for the first trip of the year. The trail grades are moderate for the most part, and are well-marked and maintained, minimizing confusion. Furthermore, the loop takes you to trail shelters, which eliminates the need for toting a tent. Head up the valley of Tea Creek to spend your first night in a pretty clearing by a great swimming hole. Then follow the Right Fork Tea Creek along an old railroad grade up to Gauley Mountain. Take a side trip to Tea Creek Meadow for great views, then cruise the crest of Gauley Mountain to another trail shelter 4,400 feet high. Loop back around Tea Creek valley and enjoy more views before dropping back down to Tea Creek Campground.

Start your loop on the Williams River Trail. Follow this old road over Tea Creek on a wooden bridge. Continue forward past the bridge, and intersect the Tea Creek Mountain Trail at 0.1 mile. Turn left on the Tea Creek Mountain Trail and trace it a mere 80 feet before turning left again on the Tea Creek Trail. Immediately begin to switchback on a footpath uphill, far above Tea Creek. Drop back down and begin to parallel Tea Creek, walking upstream among old meanders created by flooding. Cross a side stream on a wood bridge at 0.9 mile. A preponderance of rhododendron now lies between the trail and Tea Creek. Pass through a field at mile 1.1, then another clearing at mile 1.4. Old rusty tubs and pots indicate this second clearing was once inhabited. Cross Lick Creek at mile 1.7.

The trail becomes pinched in by Tea Creek on your left and a steep bank on your right. Look for wet weather falls coming from outcrops on the bank.

Fallen rocks from above crowd the path in places. Notice the large boulders in Tea Creek.

Come to a trail shelter in a clearing surrounded by yellow birch at mile 2.8. This is your first night's destination. The shelter overlooks Tea Creek. Just downstream is a deep pool, ideal for dipping.

Start day two by walking a short distance up the Tea Creek Trail to a junction. Turn right on the North Face Trail. Begin a mild ascent along an old railroad grade which passes directly behind the shelter. The wide grade is muddy in spots. After a half mile, at mile 3.3 of your loop hike, come to the Right Fork

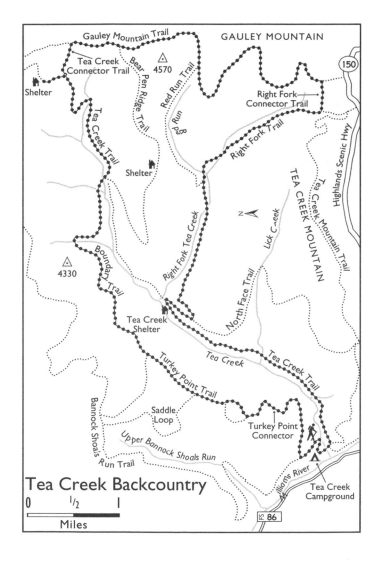

Tea Creek Backcountry

0   ½   1
Miles

Trail. Turn left on the Right Fork Trail and walk up another grade. The trail is rocky, as is the entire mountainside, and stays far above Right Fork Tea Creek. Leave the old railbed at times, walking on berms of soil to bypass muddy spots. Right Fork comes into view at mile 4.5. Soon after, work your way across a washed-out section of the railbed on a footlog. At mile 4.8, rock-hop over Right Fork, then come to a junction at mile 5.1. The Red Run Trail splits left; you stay forward on the Right Fork Trail. Step over Red Run, then climb alongside Right Fork.

At mile 5.5, cross the much smaller Right Fork, then enter a clearing surrounded by spruce, which has increased in number with the increase in elevation. Meadows and beaver dams become common features on Right Fork. Come to a trail junction at mile 6.7. For a good view turn right, staying on the Right Fork Trail and take a short side trip to Tea Creek Meadow. This clearing offers views of Gauley Mountain. Return to the junction and take the Right Fork Connector Trail to intersect the Gauley Mountain Trail at mile 7.3.

Turn left on the Gauley Mountain Trail. You are now over 4,200 feet in elevation. This old grade leads moderately up the west slope of Gauley Mountain. Cross a wooden bridge and pass through clearings at mile 8.3 and mile 9.0. Soon begin a downgrade, coming to the Red Run Trail at mile 9.5.

Keep forward on the Gauley Mountain Trail. The canopy is more open now, and the path lined with grass. Patches of rhododendron appear. Negotiate some muddy spots and come to the Bear Pen Ridge Trail at mile 10.6. Stay north on Gauley Mountain and come to the Tea Creek Connector Trail at mile 11.1. Turn left on the Tea Creek Connector Trail, walking above a railroad grade on a berm of soil removed when the grade was made. Come to the upper Tea Creek Trail at mile 11.7. Turn right and make the sharpest climb of the day up to a trail shelter at mile 12.0. This is your second night's destination. This structure looks over a small flat encircled by woods. Non-native red pines have been planted here. A spring lies behind the 4,400 foot shelter.

Start day three by returning 0.3 mile down the Tea Creek Trail. Turn right at the junction here, passing through a young spruce forest. Watch for pieces of coal and railroad ties on the trail, which make a sharp switchback to the left, then cross Tea Creek on a wooden bridge at mile 13.0 of your loop. Keep descending along the south bank of Tea Creek, which drops off to your right. Some parts of the grade here have been washed out. Closely parallel Tea Creek just before merging into a meadow at mile 13.8. Look for a beaver pond off to your left. Come to the Boundary Trail at mile 14.0. Turn right here and rock hop Tea Creek, make a brief climb, then cross a small stream coming in from your right. The Boundary Trail mildly ascends on a grade, passing a big boulder fallen from a stone bluff at mile 14.6.

The grade becomes nearly level. A road intersects from your right at mile 15.5. Continue forward on the grade a short distance, then follow the blue diamond marked trail left on a footpath into a dark and dense spruce thicket. The root- and rock-strewn trail swings around the left side of a knob and comes to the national forest boundary line at mile 16.1. This boundary is marked by red painted blazes on trees.

Parallel the boundary and climb a knob on Turkey Mountain with obscured views. Come to the Saddle Loop Trail at mile 16.8. Walk just a short distance to your left for a first-rate view of the Tea Creek watershed from a rock outcrop. The Right Fork valley is dead ahead. Tea Creek Mountain lies across the gulf.

Keep forward, now on the Saddle Loop Trail. Descend on a footpath. Keep an eye peeled on the blue diamonds marking the way, as the trail bed is not obvious. A series of sharp switchbacks begin at mile 17.2. The trail levels out at the Turkey Point Trail at mile 17.4. Turn left on the Turkey Point Trail, passing a clearing at mile 17.7. Come to the split in the Turkey Point Trail at mile 18.0. Keep forward, watching on your left for an outcrop with another good view into

Tea Creek. Intersect to the Turkey Point Connector Trail in 0.2 mile.

Turn left on the Turkey Point Connector Trail. Keep your foot on the brakes as the Jeep trail drops off the mountainside nearly 1,000 feet in a little more than a mile. Other Jeep trails merge into the main trail, but the primary route is obvious. Watch for the reddish brown trunks of the many fallen pin cherry trees. Pick up a more sane grade at mile 19.5, and keep descending, coming to the Bannock Shoals Run Trail at mile 19.9. Turn left in a clearing and emerge into the upper section of Tea Creek Campground at mile 20.1. Walk down the campground road to the hiker parking area, completing your loop at mile 20.4.

Directions: From Marlinton, drive north on US 219 for 7.0 miles to Highland Scenic Highway. Turn left on Highland Scenic Highway and follow it south for 10.0 miles to Forest Service Road 86. Head north a short distance on FS 86 to Tea Creek Campground on your right. The trailhead is just across a bridge over the Williams River at the entrance to the campground.

Contact Information

Monongahela National Forest Headquarters
200 Sycamore Street
Elkins, WV 26241
(304) 636-1800
www.fs.fed.us/r9/mnf

Cheat Ranger District Office
P.O. Box 368
Parsons, WV 26287
(304) 478-3251

Gauley Rnager District Office
Box 110
Richwood, WV 26261
(304) 846-3695

Greenbrier Ranger District Office
Box 67
Bartow, WV 24920
(304) 456-3335

Marlinton Ranger District Office
P.O. Box 210
Marlinton, WV 24954-0210
(304) 799-4334

Potomac Ranger District Office
HC 59, Box 240
Petersburg, WV 26847
(304) 257-4488

White Sulphur Springs District Office
410 East Main Street
White Sulphur Springs, WV 24986
(304) 536-2144

Cranberry Mountain Nature Center
P.O. Box 110
Richmond, WV 26261
(304) 653-4826

Seneca Rocks Discovery Center
P.O. Box 13
Seneca Rocks, WV 26884
(304) 567-2827

Monongahela Reading List

Best In Tent Camping: West Virginia, by Johnny Molloy. Menasha Ridge Press, Birmingham, Alabama, 2000.

West Virginia Hiking Trails, by Allen De Hart. Appalachian Mountain Club Books, Boston, Massachusetts, 1997.

Hiking Guide to the Allegheny Trail, West Virginia Scenic Trails Association, Charleston, West Virginia.

Smithsonian Guides to Natural America: West Virginia, Kentucky and Tennessee, edited by Bruce Hopkins. Smithsonian Institution, 1996.

Wildwater West Virginia: Streams and Creeks of the Mountain State, by Paul Davidson. Menasha Ridge Press, 1995.

Index